AWAY UP
THE NORTH FORK

AWAY UP

THE

NORTH FORK

A Girl's Search for
Home in the Wilderness

Annie Chappell

SHE WRITES PRESS

Published 2022
Printed in the United States of America
Print ISBN: 978-1-64742-269-1
E-ISBN: 978-1-64742-270-7
Library of Congress Control Number: 2022913046

For information, address:
She Writes Press
1569 Solano Ave #546
Berkeley, CA 94707

She Writes Press is a division of SparkPoint Studio, LLC.

Book design by Stacey Aaronson

For Mom and Dad, who guided me through this journey with understanding and endless love.

"I went to the woods because I wished to live deliberately, to front only the essential facts of life, and see if I could not learn what it had to teach, and not, when I came to die, discover that I had not lived..."
—HENRY DAVID THOREAU, *Walden ch. 2 (1854)*

"If you talk to the animals, they will talk with you and you will know each other. If you do not talk to them, you will not know them and what you do not know, you will fear. What one fears, one destroys."
—CHIEF DAN GEORGE, Tsleil-Waututh Nation, British Columbia, Canada, *Talk to Animals, 1974*

"Those who contemplate the beauty of the earth find reserves of strength that will endure as long as life lasts. There is something infinitely healing in the repeated refrains of nature — the assurance that dawn comes after night, and spring after winter."
—RACHEL CARSON, *Sense of Wonder* 1965

PROLOGUE

*I*n Norse mythology, Valhalla was an enormous, majestic hall ruled over by the Norse god, Odin. When warriors died in victorious battles, they were led to Valhalla by Valkyries, or spirits. Synonyms for Valhalla include Paradise, Utopia, Nirvana and Heaven.

Bill Atkinson called his place in Montana Val Halla (Bill's spelling), as a nod to the mystical land of fallen warriors; his own version of paradise.

✗

CHAPTER ONE

*M*y duffel was packed with a hand-me-down plaid wool shirt from my oldest brother, overalls, hiking boots, mittens, long underwear, some turtleneck shirts and sweaters, and my teddy bear. I wasn't going to leave Teddy behind.

It was the beginning of my senior year at Emma Willard School, a girls' boarding school in Troy, New York, but I was leaving to track down a mountain man named Bill whom I'd met only once. All I knew was that he lived on the Canadian border in Montana, and I'd booked a flight to Great Falls even though he hadn't given me an explicit invitation to come visit.

I'd met Bill over spring break of my junior year when I was home in Denver for a couple of weeks, hanging out with my friend Cini Carson. We'd just arrived back at her house after a ski weekend in the Arapahoe Basin area with two other girls.

Cini and I had met a couple summers earlier, when we were fourteen, on a student trip to France, and became close friends. Now we were enjoying some independence, our parents having given us permission to spend a weekend in a condo that belonged to the family of one of the other girls on the trip. We were without chaperones, and felt very grown-up and responsible. We took advantage of our freedom, enjoying drinking a case of Watney's Red Barrel beer (courtesy of Cini's folks), staying up late and getting stoned, and listening to Neil Young, Joni Mitchell, Blind Faith, and The Rolling Stones.

The two of us were hanging out in her family's sunroom when we heard Cini's parents talking to someone in the next room and the three adults wandered in. They introduced us to Bill. The afternoon light poured through the picture window, creating a vivid contrast between the bright warmth and the shadowed corners. I felt suddenly disoriented and overwhelmed by the image of this man in buckskins decorated with strips of beadwork over the shoulders. He smelled of wood smoke and seemed to have appeared from a different era. His presence filled the narrow room.

We had barely met before he sat down at the upright piano and started to play with such passion that I felt my insides being shot through with the music. I recognized the piece as Beethoven's "Moonlight Sonata," and I was struck by the strange juxtaposition of that elegant music and the bearded mountain man playing it. My insides felt charged and urgent, and those feelings only intensified when I saw him lost in his music, enveloped by the smell of smoke-tanned buckskins.

Bill was wild in a way I could sense but couldn't grasp, and he seemed out of his element. I guessed that he had some business with Cini's parents, Tom and Diane; they owned an art gallery in downtown Denver that sold fine western art and high-quality American Indian turquoise and silver jewelry.

The last notes faded and Bill grinned, seemingly pleased with himself. He turned around on the piano bench and started to talk about his world. When I caught Cini's attention, she raised her eyebrows in a "Wow, who *is* this guy??" kind of way. Her mom sat on a porch chair on the other side of Bill and her dad leaned against the open entry to the living room. Bill told us he'd driven his pickup from Montana to Denver to sell some of his engraved elk antler medallions, and had found the Carson Gallery. He'd hoped to buy a wolf pup in the Aspen area but that hadn't worked out, so he would be heading back to his cabin in another day or so.

I was captivated and could have listened to him recount his adventures all day. The previous summer he had taken a 600-mile trek on horseback from his cabin in Montana to Yellowstone Park through the Bob Marshall Wilderness, and he described in detail how he was forced to kill a mountain lion with his Hawken rifle, a muzzle-loader gun that allows only one shot since it has to be packed with powder and a ball. As the mountain lion bounded downhill toward him, he aimed and fired and the cat dropped to the ground, killed with a shot to the chest.

As Bill described his rugged lifestyle near the Canadian border, a picture of his 1914 homesteader's cabin next to the river and across from the jagged peaks of Glacier Park formed in my mind. Wishing the moments would slow, I sat transfixed as he shared the details of his wilderness world. I was too intimidated to interrupt him with questions, and considered how I might reach him in some other way. Maybe I could write to him, or even visit his homestead. I was convinced that the window of time was closing for changing the path of modern culture to being more aligned with something that more closely represented harmony with nature.

His Mountain Man image invoked scenes of living off the land, with a healthy respect for what the natural world

3

could provide. I associated this "back to the land" lifestyle with what I understood to that point about Native American society.

In 1962, when I was six years old, my family visited Mesa Verde, where Pueblo Indians had lived in cliff dwellings a thousand years earlier. The small museum had cases of pottery and tools, but I was much more interested in the diorama that depicted village life—children playing with simple hoops and sticks, women grinding corn and scraping a stretched hide, and men slicing strips of meat to dry and working on the stone construction of a cliff dwelling. I pictured myself in that scene as Mom read the interpretive information out loud about the ceremonies to celebrate the corn harvest, ward off illness, thank the deer for its meat, or bring rain. That world seemed balanced and peaceful.

The frontiersmen who established their homesteads across this country were nothing like the Pueblo Indians, but for me their ability to live off the land was equally alluring. As I listened to Bill, I sensed that his life represented something possible for me to attain—a world I might still be able to enter. The images he painted of his wilderness life were like a dream I had just awakened from, the scenes fading even as I tried to hold them.

Though I'd been raised in Denver and enjoyed an upper-middle-class life, with a country club membership and private school privileges, as a young girl I'd always daydreamed about living in a different era—something like what I read about in *Little House in the Big Woods*, by Laura Ingalls Wilder, that my godmother had given me for my ninth birthday. At night I'd sit in bed reading later than I was supposed to because I had to know: Would the cows die in the blizzard, or could Pa get them to the barn? Would the drought wipe out their meager gardens? I imagined slipping back in time to live like Laura Ingalls Wilder in a humble cabin with a loving family. I thought I could learn to shoot like Annie Oakley, and ride a horse through the deep woods. My imaginary Ma and I would sew a new dress for me for school.

I'd also grown up listening to Mom's stories about a simpler, rustic life at the cabin in the mountains west of Denver where her family had spent their summers. She often shared adages like "Waste not, want not"; "Neither borrower nor lender be"; and "A penny saved is a penny earned." Even though we had all we needed and more, Mom took nothing for granted, and waste in any capacity, whether it was food, resources, or potential, was unacceptable to her. I admired her values and adopted those tenets, because they felt right. I worried about waste—turned off lights and saved scraps of paper and material, feeling some pride in my resourcefulness. If I stayed over at a friend's house, I would try to force their dripping faucets to stop; it bothered me that water was going down the drain for no reason. Once, I turned off my older brother's stereo because he was not in the room and I thought he was wasting energy. I couldn't have been more than eight or nine; it made him so mad he chased after me. Of course, I screamed and he got in trouble.

By the time I met Bill, his world felt familiar to me because of my connection to the mountains and time spent at my mother's family cabin, where we enjoyed many summer weeks and occasional weekends throughout the year. There, we heated with wood, pumped water by hand, and picked currants to make jam. Our family had introduced electricity and indoor plumbing there, and we enjoyed certain modern conveniences and comforts like a refrigerator, radio and record player, and even electric blankets—it was a far cry from primitive. But I believed that I was skilled and tough and could live like the pioneers, and in my Laura Ingalls Wilder mind I pictured myself carrying water from the stream and helping Pa milk the cows.

In 1970, the first year Earth Day was celebrated, I was thirteen, and my fairy tale images of *Little House in the Big Woods* were overlaid with more pressing and real-life global issues. What I understood about pollution, habitat loss, racism and war, the disparity between rich and poor, the ugly history of slavery, and especially the greed and unapologetic destruction of Native American people and their tribal lands, left me feeling helpless and troubled. The lessons and books that influenced my early life were most certainly pointing me in the direction that led to Bill and his homestead in Montana that he called Val Halla. When I imagined living off the land in a cabin, my future life came into focus as certain, simple, and honest. And maybe, I thought, I might even share that life with a man I could love.

The reality was that I would head back to finish my junior year at boarding school and Bill would drive his late-'60s red Ford pickup back to his cabin without the wolf pup. But his trip to Denver had sparked a friendship with Hollis Williford, an artist and sculptor connected with the Carson Gallery, and a strong relationship with Cini's parents. He left them with some of his scrimshaw-carved elk ivories to sell at the gallery and left me with lingering thoughts of high peaks, a cozy cabin, and stepping into a whole other way of living.

The following summer, when the Carsons offered me a job at their western art gallery, I was excited to start working and to spend time with them at their gallery. My parents were pleased; I was only sixteen, and they thought fine art sales, an entirely new experience for me, would give me confidence and responsibility. Mom had studied painting in college and we had always been exposed to the arts, but this was a new world of art to explore.

I took the bus to downtown Denver for work and enjoyed talking to folks riding back and forth on the No. 6. It was an honest world, full of people who were entirely different from my parents and their country club friends. The gallery was filled with contemporary western paintings and sculpture. I was familiar with the work of masters like Rembrandt and Turner, and modern artists like Winslow Homer and Mary Cassat, and I had also seen the paintings and sculptures portraying the frontier West by Charlie Russell and Frederic Remington. But I loved this new generation of western artists—Jim Bama, Fred Meyers, Bev Doolittle, Hollis Williford, and others—producing beautiful paintings and sculpture depicting the cowboy life, the grand western landscapes, and Native American culture. I also discovered some of the older Western artists, including Delano, Caitlin, Georgia O'Keefe, Victor Higgins, Ernest Blumenschein, Gustave Baumann, and others who explored and painted western life and Native Americans from the early 1800s onward. Standing in front of these works was like looking through a window into another realm.

The culture, history, and spirit of the Southwest had always fascinated me, and at school I had delved into the study of Native Americans in the Southwest, especially the Navajo and the Hopi, who were farmers and pueblo dwellers. Working at the gallery enhanced those interests and the representation of the rugged West that I was so drawn to. As I spent more time around the jewelry, the skilled silver craft of Native American artisans held more depth for me, and I became more comfortable discussing Old Pawn Indian jewelry with clients and enjoying trust and respect from the Carsons.

That summer was a space between worlds for me—childhood and adulthood, school and home, old friends and new, work and play. Life at home was okay but felt slightly off-center: my two older brothers and sister were grown and had their own homes in the Denver and Boulder area, so I was alone with my parents. We had moved into a new house earlier that year, and as disjointed as I was about leaving my childhood home, I liked some aspects of this new space. It was in the same part of Denver but in a gated, upscale neighborhood away from the main thoroughfare on the other side of Cherry Creek where I'd grown up. My room was big enough for my old upright piano, and was on the ground level, right off the garage, with its own back door, so I had privacy.

The house was pretty, but its formality made it a bit cold. There was an emptiness to it, like a house you might visit on a tour; Mom and Dad had some beautiful antiques, but those objects had little to do with our family history, except for a few paintings that my dad's mother had collected. They owned none of the things I valued, like the Navajo rugs that were given in trade to my mom's father (we called him Pappy) when he traveled to the reservations between 1910 and 1920 to perform eye, ear, nose, and throat surgeries.

My parents' life seemed picture-perfect from the outside, but Mom and Dad were navigating a difficult time; their situation was not comfortable on many fronts. Dad's mother was failing and heading for the nursing home, and Mom, who did not believe in complaining or being sick, was exasperated by her mother-in-law's needs. I was aggravated with Mom for not considering what my grandmother Didi was feeling and facing at this point in her life. In spite of her bad hips and need to use "sticks" (a form of crutches that had cuffs at the elbows), she had always been emotionally independent and intellectually vital. Mom's father was still sturdy and able to manage life at eighty-seven, but he had to tend to my grandmother, who suffered from arteriosclerosis and was addicted to Percodan. Mom, meanwhile, was drinking through the day from a plastic cup of bourbon she kept in a cupboard in the laundry room; my oldest brother, Dos, was negotiating a dissolving marriage; and on top of settling into a new house, my parents were trying to launch an antique business. There were so many things out of their control that I sensed the distraction of this new enterprise gave them a challenge and something positive to work on together.

I watched my parents' lives but felt removed, like an observer of a dramatic show you're invested in but not quite a part of. Mostly what they did was keep to their familiar, established patterns: cocktail parties, bridge games, tennis, and all the pastimes of social Denver.

By the middle of the summer, I felt like I was starting to pull away from their world. A few times that summer my sister's husband visited Denver from their home in Boulder on business and found any way he could to spend time with me. I knew that his advances were wrong but I wanted the special attention, and felt emotionally charged by the secretive nature of our brief encounters.

The relationship with my brother-in-law was confusing. He'd begun "grooming" me when I was about twelve. I had already started smoking cigarettes and pot and sneaking Coors beer and hard liquor from my parents' supply to drink with friends, and I felt very in charge of my life in the way teenagers do. Exploring sex seemed to be part of the ritual of moving toward adulthood, and the pangs of longing and the pull of hormones were just budding for me. I thought that sexuality was a tool to get to love and I was not mature enough to know that my brother-in-law's advances were predatory.

He was fifteen years older than me and seven years older than my sister. At first it was flattering, and innocent. Then it was secret and alluring. But it also felt dirty and wrong to be involved with the man who married my sister, and it felt especially bad once their daughter was born. When I asked him if he loved me or loved my sister, he told me that he loved both of us; that I was more playful and she was the steady love that he needed and in some way we were complete, like two halves of a seed.

He would ask me to come out to the car, or down to the basement, or into the guest bed, sometimes even when my parents were in the house. I thought that he would be disappointed, and that what I believed was his love for me would disappear, if I refused him. If my parents had any notion of this, they never made an attempt to intervene. Mom may have had a sense that there was something going on, but Dad was less attuned to our moods, needs, and activities.

Somehow, I managed to avoid actual intercourse; or maybe he knew enough not to go there with me and risk pregnancy. In any event, he showed me how to satisfy his needs in other ways. It felt like very dangerous territory; I wanted to turn the clock back and never enter that door to begin with, but it was too late. His advances made me feel special, and I looked for his attention. It never occurred to me that I was not an equal part of the equation, but it did seem as if I was "servicing" him, and he did not really show true affection or attention to me. I felt ashamed and dishonest, and afraid of being found out. If my sister or parents learned about this, I knew it would hurt them deeply, and there wasn't a repair kit. I had established a way to be around my family without revealing the situation, however, and despite my feelings of guilt, it felt too confusing and too scary to try to change things, so I didn't.

As I started dealing with the advances of my brother-in-law, it felt like being caught in a stream; I was keeping my head above water but moving away from the safety of the shore. I "went steady" with other boys and hung out with the neighborhood boys who were outside my parents' circle of friends. There were the nice boys who had manners, but I got involved with the wrong crowd; apparently, I was earning myself a reputation.

My very proper and elegant grandmother, Didi, knew something about these indiscretions, although I am not sure how, since I thought my adolescent world was removed from her awareness. "My Darling, I have been hearing about some inappropriate activity with you and some of the neighborhood boys . . ." she quietly said one day while she was showing me how to do needlepoint stitchery at our house. She often corrected my diction and phrasing since she had studied acting, but this was outside of our relationship boundary. It was not quite admonition, not quite warning; she was just trying to help me see that it was a wrong path. Her words did sink in, just not enough to shift my course.

I was about fourteen then: confused, ashamed, and unhappy, and did not want to fall deeper into those feelings. I sensed that I needed to physically remove myself from the whole situation and culture or I would be swallowed by it.

But where could I go? I loved my home and my family, school and friends, and I didn't see a way to separate that from the part of my life that was already warped and damaged. We were brought up to be honest and civil, and had every opportunity afforded us in our well-heeled world in Denver. Our family and history in Colorado established us as "Pioneers of the 1860s." My parents, grandparents, and great-grandparents were and had been upstanding members of a newly forming cultural region. The roots and branches in my clan were strong; the mountains and the pioneer spirit were part of our DNA. How could I leave one part of my life and keep another?

But if I *could* start over, maybe I could get it right, and put the bad history into deep storage.

The summer before my sophomore year, Mom signed me up to join a group of Denver-area students for a trip to France where we would live with host families near Bordeaux. We were mixed in age and it was a wonderful group of musical and intelligent young adults, including Cini. We formed some tight friendships. Our mentors and chaperones gave us lots of freedom and, between the day trips and lessons, exposed us to a number of new experiences.

By the end of our journey, I'd decided that I should go away to a boarding school for girls where my new friend from that trip, Martha, was going to start in September, just a few weeks away. It would be safe, temptation-free, and I wouldn't have to negotiate my broken life at home.

Mom and Dad fully endorsed my idea, and when the school accepted me, they traveled with me to the East Coast, where we visited museums and antique shops in New York

City and spent time with Dad's sister, Joan, and her family before they drove me up and dropped me off at Emma Willard School in Troy, New York. That was the fall of 1971.

On the Fourth of July, 1973, the Carsons invited me for a backyard picnic and slideshow of photos that Hollis had taken on a visit to see Bill in Montana in June. Bill had invited Hollis to visit Val Halla when they met the previous spring through the gallery. I was excited to get closer to his Montana world and replace my imagined scenes with the real thing. The opening slide showed peaks in Glacier Park glowing with an iridescent golden light across the river from Bill's cabin. There were pictures of the horses and goats, barn, cabin, and henhouse. Bill was in some of the photos, and it was a surprise to see him dressed in blue jeans and a flannel shirt—I pictured him in buckskins—but he always wore a beaded headband holding back his shoulder-length hair and either his work boots or beaded moccasins.

Thoughts of Bill floated in and out of my mind daily. His engravings in elk ivory were kept in the case with the Indian jewelry at the Carson Gallery, and I saw them every day that I spent at work, so there was a strong presence from his world with me. I imagined myself there working beside Bill in the garden or sitting next to the river. The pictures and account of Hollis's visit stayed with me, and the idea that I might go to Montana one day seemed possible and filled my thoughts all summer.

CHAPTER TWO

*B*y the time I got back to Emma Willard for my senior year of high school, I'd been obsessively thinking for months about a life with Bill in Montana and how to get there. If I wrote to him, would he write back? I drafted a letter a dozen times in my head before I finally put it on paper.

In my letter, I explained that I understood why he had chosen to live in a remote cabin in the wilderness, apart from society, learning to survive like the early frontiersmen. He had said he'd abandoned society after returning from Vietnam in 1968, and I wrote that I respected his ability to survive in the wilderness and dreamed about the same kind of life for myself.

I was hoping to at least start a relationship on paper, and I went so far as to imagine I might get an invitation to live with him. We had only met that one time, and briefly, at the Carsons', and I'd just been a kid in the background; would he even remember me? It was naive to assume that I would have impressed him from a distance, and given the upper-class culture and capitalist society I was part of, I guessed that he would not approve of my roots or trust my sincerity. Even so, I felt certain I could show enough gumption and conviction to prove that I was not the enemy.

My letter was also a little desperate; I was looking for a way to leave behind parts of my life at home, things I no longer seemed able to manage. I was smoking too much pot and drinking as if I were an adult, and I wanted to find a way to end the involvement with my sister's husband. As a high school senior, I'd be expected to set a path for my adult life, including applying to college and becoming a contributing member of society. My classmates had high goals, good grades, and direction enough to pursue their dreams; they seemed ready for the responsibility of becoming adults, establishing careers, and raising families. I, however, felt less and less capable on that front. College and a professional career, and the intellectual realm in general, did not match my vision of the future.

Not only that, but I'd arrived at school that fall anxious that I might be pregnant from my brother-in-law, even though we hadn't quite gone all the way. That dark cloud hung over me until at last, a few weeks into school, my period arrived.

If only I could step away from that worried part of my life, and follow an entirely different path. Somehow, I needed to start over.

"Dear Mountain Man," my letter to Bill began—I wanted to sound personal but deferential. I had his mailing address from the packages of engravings he'd sent to the Carson Gallery. Along with the letter, I included a tiny piece of tanned beaver pelt that he had used to pack some carved ivories he'd shipped to the gallery—so he'd associate me with the Carsons and Hollis, or maybe as proof that I knew them.

Emma Willard School sorted our letters into a wall of mailboxes with brass faces and small windows like those in post offices from another era, and we girls eagerly made our way down to its home in the dorm basement each day to check for our mail. I scanned the contents of my own box expectantly every day. Bill would *have* to write back.

A couple of weeks after I mailed my letter, I saw the letter I'd been waiting for. There was a drawing of a crossed knife and tomahawk next to *WFA* as the return address. My heart raced.

I hurried up to my room, opened the letter, and read and reread the single-spaced front-and-back typed letter from his old Remington typewriter.

```
          postmark Oct 15, 1973—Polebridge, Montana

Whoa, Annie Chappell,
     No, I can't very well place you, and wonder
yet where the piece of one of my beaver pelts
fell into your hands. For the life of me I can't
remember cutting up that pelt, tho I recognize it
of course. Only one man skins a beaver that way,
and the tan is with chrome salts. The heavy guard
hair had been removed, making the soft under fur
so gentle to the touch. I use these special-
plucked beaver for sleeping robes, and can't ever
recall cutting one up. Where did you get it and
how? I have only tanned a couple this way, and
I'm intrigued that you returned it to me.
     So, you are aware of city living being a non-
existent means of life. I was a damn tender age
when I reached the same conclusion, and began
with a clear cut goal in mind to prepare myself
to live the wildest freest life imaginable left
to live. The terms have been harsh and cruel at
times, but the past is well learned lessons, and
now, that goal is just within my reach. The
horses await, waxing a bit fat on the fall cured
grass and hay, and after a little trip this
summer, I now have the know how necessary for
extended trips into the wildest remaining
stretches of wilderness left. I have located an
area to the north some few hundred miles that
might prove the end of a long-held dream, and
```

there is very little left to stop me from finding it.

This cabin where I now live all but answered that dream for many years. The wildest animals abound just beyond my very door. Only yesterday, I ran into a bull moose and 3 calves not a half a mile to the south west. He stood and could easily have been meat hangin' but the weather is still too warm, and meat must keep 5-6 months hanging in a cache, so I held fire. Looking for a fat bear I was, as the grease is the best for baking and cooking there is, and it is fully digestible by the human system.

I recently tanned up a bear hide, and made a new vest, as I traded Hollis my last fine beaver vest. The comfort of such a hide just can't be known unless felt. Your interest in tanning is admired, but let me caution you to seek out a perfectionist for lessons, so you won't make other's mistakes. I wasted years as a kid fooling with hides on other peoples' say so, before it became apparent only a few, a rare few, produced what they said they could.

You guessed it right about the wilds being a working life. But it is really not hard once the lessons are learned. Nothing is hard once the initial gleaning of its secret is worked out, but the cruel fact is teachers are damn few and far apart, and those that know are so far removed from the non-existence, they can't be found. Nor do they want to be found. I pride myself on my seclusion and privacy, tho I am easily accessible as of now, when the road is open, which is most of the summer. But when the ghost face covers the land, his silent blanket of white excludes all. Now tho, they have started using snow mobiles, and so I must go further north up into the further reaches of mountains that will never know the whine of man and his machines.

That place has been found. The dream of

dreams, a high mountain valley with but one entrance, and that miles from the nearest tread of wheels. Elk abound, but all game leaves in the fall, as the valley is too high, the snows too deep. It commands absolute seclusion from all the sight and sound of the outside world.

Perhaps I will be in Denver this Xmas, as I wish to do further promoting of my work. The Carsons are the finest of people, and Hollis is a true artist and fine friend. Also, friend Paul has an abode somewhere I never heard of called Arvada, that must be near the Denver area, as he was there when I made my appearance last March. Hadn't seen each other since '63, no '66. Friends I have but few, and cherish these immensely, so prehaps a Xmas trek would be enjoyable. But, do I hate the necessity of appearing to further my work. Soon now, it won't be necessary, as something is in the making that will get the word out that there is an existence far removed from the realm of time and material gathering of shackles.

An elk roast is steaming up the shack and the Dutch oven is filled to overflowing with steaming vegetables. Red meat is a mountain man's delight, and this child is ravenous just now. This is the finest time for living in the mountains. The hush before Ghost Face seals all the forest in cold ice and snow. Game meat is plentiful, root cellar full, fruit canned, flour stored. A time to eat and enjoy it to the fullest, for aren't we all but what we eat?

Now I know, this piece of beaver was used for packing ivory medallions, yes?? Did you keep it for awhile as I see your post mark is NY? I still don't remember cutting that pelt up.

Regards,
W.F. Atkinson

It was not exactly an invitation to join him, but it wasn't a closed door either. If I could just get to Bill's cabin, then I could sort out my new life with him.

There were lots of logistics to figure out if I was going to go to Montana. Undoubtedly the school would treat this as outright rebellion, but that would all be behind me once I left. I'd have to go before winter arrived, sometime before November, and I'd have to find Bill's cabin. I called the airport in Albany to find out which airlines flew to Montana, and the decision was made for me. The closest I could get to Bill's cabin was Great Falls, which was south and east of him by about two hundred and fifty miles. From there I could probably hop a bus to Kalispell, south of Val Halla by about eighty miles. He'd mentioned logging trucks, so it didn't seem unreasonable that I could hitchhike from Kalispell.

Since I couldn't phone home for money and didn't have enough cash to buy my airplane ticket, I figured I would go door to door around the dorms to solicit contributions from lots of people. That way I wouldn't be too indebted to any one girl. It worked. When my dorm mates opened their doors, I led on that I was in some kind of trouble I couldn't talk about, and since we could all imagine that kind of trouble, they all gave me $5 donations without asking too many questions.

I wondered endlessly about whether Bill would welcome me, so I wrote to tell him that I *had* to live the wilderness life. In my naivete, I figured he would simply accept me into his world.

My parents were a primary consideration. I would need to assure them that this was okay, and not to worry. I had talked about Bill with them from the moment I met him. Now I sent them a brief and intentionally vague letter about my plans, and included a quote from him that endorsed my reason to pursue that lifestyle:

Oct. 20, 1973

Dear Mom and Dad,

I AM IN ECSTACY!! I wrote to Mountain Man, saying that I know how to speak French (for he's voyaging to Paris) and that I'm learning how to skin and tan animal hides, and that I'd like to live with him. I put the beaver fur in the envelope and he replied that he couldn't remember cutting the pelt up and wondered how all the guard hairs came out of it . . .

"So, you are aware of city living being a non-existent means of life. I was a damn tender age when I reached the same conclusion, and began with a clear cut goal in mind to prepare myself to live the wildest freest life imaginable left to live . . ."

I have got to live up there in the wilds—I'll go nuts if I don't— I'm willing to give up city life anytime now, and go live in the wild, white wilderness of Montana. This probably sounds futile to you because you spent your lives working hard towards where we are now, and at this point I want to discard all of civilization . . .

—love you dearly and truly,
Annie xoxoxxxooxxo

The taxi pulled into the school drive through the iron gates and waited. My four friends and I quietly left through a side door where we knew few people would see us. These four knew about my plan and were helping me pack up and make my break for the wilderness. Susan had cut my hair short so it would be easier to take care of, since Bill's cabin would not have running water. Martha gave me a drawing of a person on horseback coming around the side of the mountain. Lisa and Jackie encouraged me to be brave. We were romantic teenagers who valued conviction and a sense of adventure. This certainly qualified, and my friends supported my haphazard plan.

All five of us rode in the taxi to the airport, in so doing missing a student council meeting (Jackie and I were members, and Martha was class president). The ride from Troy to the Albany airport was charged with the sense of doing something illicit and daring. Adrenaline kept me from looking back, and I smiled to cover my fear.

I boarded the plane headed west and took a deep breath on the ascent, trying to settle the nervous flutter in my stomach. As the landscape patterns shifted below, I thought about how my world was about to change because of that chance encounter with Mountain Man Bill six months earlier.

At Chicago's O'Hare airport, I had to change planes. After I debated about calling someone in my family, I decided to call my older sister to let her know where I was headed and that I would be alright. Jen had always looked out for me, and I trusted her to understand how I felt. I also wanted the comfort of her voice before going to a remote cabin without a phone.

"Hi Jen, it's Binks." I never called her from school, so this was odd.

"Where are you?" she asked. "It's the middle of the day . . ."

"I'm in Chicago, at the airport. I'm going to Montana to live with the Mountain Man I told you about—Bill." I had told Jen about Bill right after I first met him at Cini's house. She'd understood the intrigue, but had no idea about my intent. "I have to get there before it starts to snow," I rationalized.

"You're doing what? But why?"

I knew she thought there had to be something more compelling to explain this sudden impulse of mine, but there was no way I could describe what I was running away from, so I wanted to sound certain about what I was running to.

"I *have* to live in the wilderness, and Bill will be able to teach me survival skills. It's my one chance, since he said he might leave to move further north. I have to go now or I won't find him."

"Are you sure you want to do this, Binks? I mean, it seems pretty risky . . . Do Mom and Dad know?"

It took a second or two to steady my voice, to try to sound sure-footed. Finally, I said, "No, but I wrote them a letter. It'll get there in couple of days. I'm sure they'll call you when they get it. When you do talk to them, tell them I'm okay, and that I'll be fine, and I'll write soon—"

The operator came on the line of the pay phone to warn us that time was up.

"Bye, Jen, I love you."

"Bye, Binks, be careful. I love you too."

In this second letter that I'd sent to Mom and Dad to let them know that I was leaving for Montana, I'd purposely waited to send it so they could not put a stop to my plan. I had included Bill's postal address so they could reach me, and I was confident that it would explain everything, justify my journey. I thought those few sentences would address their fears. My parents had different ideas about what a young girl with our means should aim for, so I had to convince them that all would be well, and this was a good idea.

Oct. 25, 1973

Dear Mom and Dad,

You both know about Mountain Man, he's a fine person, and the moment I saw him I knew that I wanted to share his life—but now is when I have to go, to wait would be a mistake because he is soon going further north, and I must get there before the snow flies . . .

I explained to them that I was not running away—that this was an adventure—and expressed that they should not be worried about me. "I hope I'm like a little sister to Bill, at least for the time being," I wrote. I signed off with two x's and promised to be home for Christmas.

The plane landed at the Great Falls airport, a one-story, open room that looked more like a small train station than an airport. As I walked across the tarmac toward the door, I could hear that I was being paged. My heart raced; of course it was my parents.

The woman at the ticket counter pointed me to the phone booth just past the handful of long benches in the room. Everything about the situation seemed urgent; I felt panicked as I neared the phone booth and mentally assembled an apology for causing such trouble. I pushed back against the tightness in my throat and the rush of unsettled thoughts vying for attention. How would I get to Bill, and what was I going to be up against if I did (given that he would not necessarily have received the letter, sent only a few days earlier, in which I'd let him know I was on my way)? And now, with my parents on the phone, how would I face the consequences of leaving school and explain my rationale to them?

"Hi, Mom and Dad."

"Annie! Do you know what you've done?! What were you thinking?" I could hear the distress in Mom's voice. "What if something were to go wrong while you are in the middle of nowhere? What if you got appendicitis?"

Mom was especially worried about this. She would occasionally relate her own frightening experience with developing appendicitis while at the cabin with her family when she was in her teens, and they'd all had to rush to get her back to Denver on rough dirt roads, which took about three hours in those days.

"The school called us this morning and said, 'We have lost your daughter.'" Mom was pretty wound up. "We thought you were dead!" Then she chuckled a little and some of the tension was relieved.

"Really?" *That was a strange way to inform my parents,* I thought.

Mom explained that the person she'd spoken to at the school had apparently known that I was going to find someone called Mountain Man. When the school discovered that I was gone, the only logical conclusion was for them to press my friends, who were genuinely concerned about me. What were my friends supposed to do? I never felt betrayed. Even I was questioning the wisdom of my actions.

Mom and Dad had immediately called the Carsons,

who'd told them that Bill lived on the Canadian border, twenty-three miles north of the little store and post office in Polebridge, Montana. They'd then called the Polebridge outpost to find out more about him. It seemed Bill had built quite a reputation for himself. "He fucks his goats!" Mom exclaimed with alarm.

"Mom!! No he doesn't!" I had *never* heard her use foul language other than "damn," so this caught my attention.

Dad sounded like he was more in control, but I could tell he was confused and upset. "Babesy, we don't understand why you are doing this. There are lots of people who are concerned, and you have been entirely thoughtless. We know you have your reasons, but this is not well-considered. We don't know him, and neither do you."

They urged me to come home and talk things over for a few days. I pushed through the fog in my head to get my bearings. It made some sense to go home; then, if I ended up leaving for Montana at a later date, it would be with a better plan and I could avoid wreaking more emotional havoc on my family. I was relieved in the way of a criminal who wants to get caught to save them from a more terrible outcome.

It was three o'clock in the afternoon, and the next flight from Great Falls to Denver was not until the following morning around 9:00 a.m., so I had the evening and through the night to think things over on the wooden bench that would be my island for those next hours. And I had Teddy, who served as my pillow that night. I felt dread about going home; my plan had failed, and I had caused an enormous amount of grief for Mom and Dad. Now what?

᠅

It was a long evening, and a restless night for me as I thought about what I was doing and why. I loved my parents deeply and was so sorry to have hurt them. Throughout my childhood I'd had a close relationship with them both. I'd always felt grateful to be their child, and I relied on them being present in my life. My need to break away from the world I'd been raised in was at odds with all they had wished for me, which was hard on all of us.

Mom and Dad were caring, intelligent people, admired by their friends and family, and respected in the community. They had upper-class manners, and I'd always watched with interest how they interacted with their friends, family, and the folks they hired to help around the house.

They'd given their four kids everything we needed, and they'd made a point of instilling the values—honesty, compassion, generosity, and hard work—that they deemed critical to being a decent person. I was a lucky kid with a family that had come fully equipped with privilege and social status, and with freedom from want.

They rarely punished me; we were admonished rather than scolded. They would tell me to stop whining, or that I was acting spoiled. I would be reminded, on our way to a party or cultural event, to behave like a lady. Whenever they hosted a cocktail party, which seemed like a regular affair, they insisted that I politely greet their friends with a handshake, then keep my hands behind my back while they spoke. And I believed that it was right to model their ideal behavior.

But there were pockets of discomfort between my parents. Their public veneer of civility was occasionally pulled aside in private, exposing their less-than-perfect relationship. Things broke down with alcohol, which was a constant presence at home. The glass of wine at dinner was the middle course between the cocktail at five, and the sips from the bottle after dinner lasted into the evening. Alcohol caused grief and had great power. I'd seen how it could change people, and it had seeped in and found its place in my life.

Mom often drank to the point of sloppy starting at 5:00 p.m. She tucked me in every night, and by the time I was six or so, I realized that most nights she'd had too much to drink. She would go from competent and clear to unsteady and maudlin, kind of weepy, and sometimes bitter. From the time I was very young, she would come to my room repeatedly at bedtime to kiss me good night. It was more than uncomfortable. I never invited any of my friends to stay over, and I often farmed myself out to stay overnight at their houses. One night, when I was ten or eleven, Mom picked me up at a friend's house about a mile from home. She was weaving the station wagon from side to side on our neighborhood streets; when the car bounced off a curb I finally insisted she stop and let me drive the last four blocks home, though I was barely able to reach the gas and brake. I got us into the driveway and helped her to bed.

On occasion Mom and Dad would fight, and it upset me in ways I couldn't voice. Once or twice, it was vicious. I watched from the top of the stairs one night when they were arguing and pushing at each other near the front door at the bottom of the stairs. I ran down, thinking I could get between them and fix what seemed so broken. I don't know where my brothers and sister were that night, but certainly they'd had their own interactions like this with our parents. There were a handful of days when Mom wore her sunglasses all day because she "ran into the door," and no one ever talked about what had really happened.

During the day, when Mom was sober, she was a good

pal, and I absorbed our positive or happy times together because they seemed special, but also fleeting. When I was young, she would play hide-and-seek with me or help me procure the wallpaper and bits of fabric I needed to outfit my cardboard box troll house. We went to the library at least once a week and I would bring home a huge pile of books to read at the kitchen table while she cooked. Some nights she would sing a lullaby, or her version of one. When she sang it felt like something that she shared only with me.

Mom was one of the role models I wanted to emulate. She embodied attitude and had some skills of the pioneer women and the life that attracted me, and she'd broken free of some of the upper-class expectations. I watched and sometimes helped when she sat on the ground in her jeans, white shirt, and work gloves and laid all the bricks in the patio. And she taught me how to saw a board and hammer a nail when we made a bench together for the utility room. She built the stone walls and steps at our cabin, and sometimes liked to brag about how she'd won the softball throw in elementary school, beating the boys. Her hands were rough and she proudly called them "working hands."

She was also extremely organized, and kept our family photos and histories in a tidy array of albums. There was not a closet or drawer with any extraneous anything. She often got rid of things that she considered clutter, like toys. When I came home from camp and my trolls, and their house that I'd built, AND their turquoise Tonka jeep, were gone, I panicked. "Mom, where are the trolls?!?" She gave the answer I feared: "Well, Babesy, aren't you too old to be playing with dolls?" I was heartbroken. Pet fish, turtles, clothes, and (only sometimes) books also disappeared over the years.

Mom had an amazing memory, an analytical mind, and

a sense of propriety. She was a stickler for proper grammar. When news reporters said something like "There are less people in the city" she would correct them from her spot on the couch, "There are FEWER people in the city!" (I got that same nudgy tendency from her; to this day, I cringe when I hear a sentence that ends with a preposition.)

Mom and Dad played bridge a couple of nights a week, and Mom played weekly games with her bridge club during the day. She was sharp and would often win a few dollars from her friends. As a high school student, she'd excelled in math, especially geometry, and had always loved puzzles.

But her truest ability was drawing and painting. Her landscape and portrait paintings from the '40s and '50s were well crafted and organized, simple and handsome—imagine a blend of Georgia O'Keefe, Edward Hopper, and an artful paint-by-number style. She did not paint much when I was growing up, however, and had lots of excuses for that, mostly about having to do laundry and cook instead.

I admired my dad and thought his work seemed noble and honest. My father was the president of a small manufacturing business in Denver along the Platte River that made iron lungs and respirators. He wore a suit and tie when he left for the office with his briefcase, and the ubiquitous brimmed hat that all men wore then. He worked hard, and believed in hard work. It was important to him to provide us with a good education, travel, exposure to the arts, and solid social standing. He also expected that we would meet his standards: behave properly, dress well, and excel in school. He valued words, and language in any form; literacy was a source of pride and interest in our family, and Dad especially enjoyed playful constructions like spoonerisms, limericks, theater, and song lyrics. Music was also a big part of our life. Dad made sure we had a decent stereo system and a cabinet full of records of all sorts.

Dad's glass was half full, and his happiness spilled over when he was engaged in the things he enjoyed entirely. He was a good fly fisherman. He and Mom loved nothing more than to explore a special stretch on one of the western rivers, away from the rest of the world, and share a tin cup of bourbon near the fire at the end of the day. He loved sweets, good wine, and rich food (especially French cooking), so he suffered from gout and always carried just a little extra weight. He was affable, and he often chatted with people he'd just met as if they were pals. When he was pleased, he would say, "Oh, that's swell!" or "Just grand!" or "Say now, that's terrific." And he had endearing names for his children, at least for me and my sister. I was the Babes, or Babesy, or Ansy Pansy. Jen was Petunia, or Petune, or Juniper.

When I was very young Dad seemed stern and I was a little nervous around him. He was not entirely comfortable with small children, and there was no cuddle or story time with him. He was handsome, intelligent, and proper, but he had a very sentimental core that was never far below his fatherly facade, and when he laughed or cried or sang he was sweet and vulnerable and the sternness disappeared.

Once I was a little older and started testing limits, Dad did not let anything slide. If I let him down and he felt he needed to address my behavior, we would have a "talk," which I dreaded. It always seemed to start, "Now, Babesy, I am very disappointed in you . . ." He was not unkind, though, and I understood that he was simply trying to guide me. This time, I knew that I had gone beyond disappointing him, and his troubled heart was my fault.

When the nine o'clock boarding time finally arrived, I

was still running these loops of memories and the probable scenario that would take place when I faced Mom and Dad through my head. It would be a relief to just get the initial few hours behind us. I tried to construct what I would say to them, but it was an exhausting exercise with no clear end.

CHAPTER THREE

As the plane set down in Denver, I grew even more anxious about seeing my parents, wondering how I'd negotiate on this unsteady ground. It was not as simple as an apology. I walked down the ramp into the terminal and felt a flood of comfort, shame, and vulnerability when I saw my parents waiting for me. Mom and Dad were relieved to have me home, but their deeper anxieties were evident. The half-hour car ride was quiet, but tense; though they weren't angry, none of us was sure how to sort our feelings. We would discuss things when we got home.

Mom understood my desire to find solitude and the simple life in the mountains but warned me that leaving high school was out of the question—that it would be a huge mistake. Dad was not going to scold me, but I knew we would have a "talk."

"Dear, you have caused your mother and me enormous concern about you," he told me when we sat down together in the library. "We are *terribly* troubled about this. Do you understand the distress you have put others through at school? Do you realize that you are being selfish?"

His words felt like icicles stabbing my heart. I knew I had worried them, and unsettled the routine of home and family. It cut to the core of my being and left me with a deep soul-ache to cause such grief, but I wanted them to see that I needed to go to Montana, and that I was in fact trying to consider the future, even if I couldn't fully grasp it. There was so much that I could not open up to them about. I could not explain how heartsick I was about the mess I was in with my brother-in-law, and I didn't think I should try to untangle the knots of alcohol and pot and how out of control I felt with them. They had their own issues with alcohol, and it was all much too complicated to address, so I just kept those troubling issues inside the lockbox.

I knew I had to present a clearheaded rationale, and let them know that I was carefully weighing my options, even though I felt unsteady.

Until now, I had not been a troublemaker, at least not as far as Mom and Dad were concerned. They saw me as independent, social, compassionate, and lively. There hadn't ever been much occasion to push against them, or even to argue with them, because they were so accommodating. When alcohol started to affect their interactions after dinner most evenings, I simply avoided them. And when I had adventures that would not meet their approval, I just didn't tell them. They trusted me to act appropriately, and to approach adulthood gracefully.

As it turned out, the headmaster from Emma Willard, Dennis Collins, was coming to Denver that week before the long Halloween weekend to do some recruiting and fundraising for the school—a strange coincidence. Mom had offered to host a tea and slide show for prospective students and their parents, and I couldn't avoid being part of the event. No doubt I would need to address the consequences of leaving school with Mr. Collins. He happened to be staying nearby with the family of a girl who had graduated the previous year from Emma Willard, so we set up a meeting. It felt very official.

"Well, Annie," he greeted me when I walked into the house where he was staying, "I hadn't thought that I would see you in Denver, but it seems you had an adventure in mind." It was a friendly opening.

Mrs. Coleman escorted us to their library and left us alone.

Mr. Collins sat down behind the desk and continued. "What were you planning to do if you got to Montana?"

"I need to live in the wilderness," I answered in the most broad, nebulous kind of way.

"That doesn't tell me much," he pushed. "What does that hold for you? Don't you want to go to college? You have put your senior year—well actually, your future—in jeopardy."

I'd known I would get that reminder.

"I belong in the mountains, so no, I don't want to go to college." I gave him a description of our cabin and explained my deep connection there. "It's where I feel happy. At home." I threw in some jumbled and slightly teary justification for going back to the land because the world was such a mess, and because I really *was* worried about the future. I tried to sound positive and certain about my need to live in the mountains instead of pursuing college and a career, but my confusion and apprehension were evident.

"Don't you think it would be wise to finish your senior year, in case you come back and decide you want to go to college?" He was leading, but doing so gently. "If you're so concerned about the environment, wouldn't it be more important to stay in school so you can work on those issues that you care about?" This was a good insight, and it resonated with me, though it conflicted with my determination to *not* go to college.

"Yes, I guess so." This was the answer Mom and Dad wanted me to give, but I also knew it made sense not to squander the chance to finish school.

I would be on probation for the rest of the semester and there would be some extra work to catch up with studies. It was close to the end of October, and I would either have to get back to school to take the SAT by November 3 or find a way to take it in Denver, then go back to school.

Mr. Collins considered my situation and came up with a plan. "Here's what I suggest, Annie. Actually, it's an assignment. Before you come back to school in a week or so, I want you to spend a few days at your family cabin—alone or with your little dog, Josie." I was grateful that he was listening and understood what I was reaching for.

"You need to experience the solitude at your cabin and think things over before coming back to school. Can you arrange that?"

"Okay," I said. As I pictured the cabin, I felt my breath slow; I was relieved to have some certainty about the next week. I promised that I would study hard, since I could now be suspended for anything resembling errant behavior or poor grades, and my headmaster gave me the nod; just like my parents, he would trust me to behave like an adult.

Later that week I got a note from my housemother, Mrs. Carter, expressing her concern and encouraging me to come back. She told me that they missed me—"Our corridor is dead without you!"—caught me up on a few details about the other girls, and signed off with affection: "We love you and I hope you'll be back with us."

Time at home with Mom and Dad was shadowed with

anxiety and uncertainty, so I was glad to have the directive from Mr. Collins to spend a few days alone at the cabin with Josie. My parents were equally surprised by and pleased with his suggestion and wisdom. We figured out that I could take the SAT at a nearby high school—Cini would even join me to take it—after a few days at the cabin, so that was set. Then I could get back to school.

The next morning, my brother Dos's wife, Sherry, drove me to the cabin, about an hour and a half from home. The early first dusting of snow was on the ground and it was cold, crisp, and beautiful. Sherry helped me bring in a bag of groceries and my sleeping bag and gave me a big hug and then headed home to Denver; she'd come back for me in four days.

Josie, our schnauzer-poodle mix, stayed with me wherever I went, and her company was welcome. I started a fire in the wood cookstove and waited until I could damp it down, then we spent time outside walking and cleaning up the wood pile. Our first day came to a quiet end reading by the woodstove in the kitchen.

Climbing out of bed in the chill of the morning was daunting, especially because it took some time to get the 1880 vintage Born woodstove in the kitchen lit and warm. Then I had the day to fill. I collected rosehips for tea, split some wood, crafted a simple bow and arrow (it might have startled a rabbit but had no potential to hurt anything), and took long walks around the lake with Josie. In the evenings, I concocted some strange soups on the wood stove, put an entry or two in my journal, and did a little drawing. My life was usually full of friends and family and the general business of being a high school student; this was the first time I had spent entire days alone. The solitude was not the comfortable peace I expected.

There were a few old photo albums of our family from the early 1900s onward in the cabin, and looking through them I thought about my great-great-grandparents, who were pioneers in Colorado, and the colorful characters and stories of our family. On Dad's side, I am a fourth-generation native Coloradoan; on my mom's side, a fifth. My two grandmothers were neighbors and friends, and there was a photograph of them as young girls in frocked dresses and button shoes in front of their homes in Denver, around 1900. Some of our family came west in the 1860s by wagon, carrying a dining table and hutch that we grew up with. I imagined them building log cabins, raising animals, living a hard but rewarding life in the mountains. In fact, they lived in Denver and were quite civilized at a time when Denver was a crossroads between east and west, as well as north and south along the Rockies. My family members were business leaders in mining, banking, and ranching in Colorado and New Mexico. Sometime around 1870, my great-great-grandfather on Mom's side, John Wellington Nesmith, constructed a crib dam that created Wellington Lake from three feeder streams, about sixty miles southwest of Denver at the northern edge of what is now the Pike National Forest. The lake/reservoir still serves as a water supply for Denver and Front Range sugar beet farmers. Initially, there was a small structure that served as a cook's cabin for the men who built the dam. Not long after, a larger cabin with a fireplace and two bedrooms was built adjacent to the cook's cabin, and now they are joined. The cabin would stay in our family, shared by the descendants of John Wellington Nesmith.

Sitting next to the woodstove at the kitchen table, the window over the sink allowed a view of the mountains across the lake to the south. The familiarity was welcome, but it struck me how powerful it was as a landscape. Wellington Lake sits at the base of a ridge, just below a rock outcropping (a geologic extrusion known as a batholith) of Pike's Peak granite that we had always called the Castle, about 1,500 feet above the lake, at an elevation of 9,500 feet. From the lake the Castle looks almost two-dimensional, but once among the spires and house-size boulders, it is deceptively vast and layered. I had climbed around up there a few times with older siblings or parents, enough to know it was easy to get disoriented. It felt to me as if a powerful force was embodied in that rock formation; I had the sense that some entity was breathing and watching. I imagined that the Ute Indians who lived in that region might have considered it sacred, like the Devil's Tower or the Hopi mesas—a place where the Great Spirit dwelled.

My mother's family spent their summers at the cabin, and all of my extended family had spent time since enjoying the cabin and lake and working together to cut the winter wood for the stove, build stone walls, and leave our city life behind. When I was just old enough to reach the pedals and see through the steering wheel, I learned to how drive my grandfather's 1947 Willys jeep that we kept there. It was a double-clutch vehicle, and a little complicated: you pulled the choke out all the way, turned the key to start the engine, and gave it a little gas . . . once the engine cranked on and warmed some, you pushed the choke in slowly, unhitched the brake, and off you went. Its voice was like a quieter version of a motorcycle, but more mechanical and musical.

With so much time to myself, it was comforting to think about my mother and her summertime cabin life with her mother and father and three sisters. She'd told certain stories often enough that they'd become part of my own history.

Mom was happy and completely at home in the mountains. She was the tomboy among her sisters and had often fished and camped alone at the lake when she was young; she felt comfortable with that solitude and challenge. When I looked across the lake to the Castle and the ridge above it, I imagined the scenes of Mom's favorite story about an adventure with her sister and another girl when she was about sixteen. Mom, her older sister, Isie, and their maid's granddaughter, Evelyn, climbed to the ridge behind the Castle to Needle's Eye, a rock formation with a man-size hole that you could barely see from the cabin. The elevation on that ridge was about 11,000 feet, 3,000 feet above the lake. The hiking distance along the trail was roughly eight miles, and pretty steep for much of the climb, and it was dark when they finally got to the top. It was impossible for all three of them to turn around since Evelyn was out of shape and quite afraid—so, in spite of the darkness, they decided that Isie would climb down the front of the ridge—a treacherously steep, rocky, mountainside—to the lake to let the maid, Annie, know they were safe.

It took Isie the entire night to get to the lake. Mom tried shouting to her to keep in contact, but that was soon impossible because of the tree-studded slopes and steep drainages. After a long, chilly night, Mom and Evelyn finally climbed down.

This was an adventure that Mom recounted many times. It and her other stories about time spent at the lake created another dimension of the place for me, and as a child, I often lay in bed and imagined going back in time to live like a pioneer girl in the mountains, cooking a stew on the woodstove, sewing a quilt in the winter, and picking wild strawberries and currants for jam in August.

After four days, it was time to get ready to go back to

Denver. Sherry would come up for me around noon, so I cleaned the ashes from the wood stove, turned off the water in the pump house, filled the wood box, swept the floors, and emptied the refrigerator, taking the last of my bean soup concoction to dump up the hill for whatever critters would come around. I was looking forward to Sherry's company but also a little sad to leave the cabin. It had been lonely, but I'd realized that I did feel at home with that realm, and that being alone was not terrifying, just a matter of being at ease, and productive, or creative.

CHAPTER FOUR

*T*hings had not gone as planned, but I was quietly relieved that I now had more time to figure out how and when I would get to Montana, and to make sure that Bill would accept me once I got there. I would also be able to finish school, which not only eased my parents' concern but also felt right to me; I thought I should at least complete this chapter of my life.

After I returned to Emma Willard, I felt somewhat like a hero—the celebrated rebel who'd made her stand. Classmates were curious and offered words of support. Teachers were sympathetic but also careful not to endorse what I'd done. I was treated as if I'd had a breakdown. And the money I had "borrowed" from dorm mates was never mentioned.

For my final fall semester at Emma Willard I signed up for classes that aligned with my deepest interests. I wrote papers on the Aswan Dam for a political science class, on the paintings and life of Frederic Remington for art history class, on the primate activity we observed at the Bronx zoo for anthropology, and on the Mayan ruins in Spanish for Señora Hunter. I created an independent study with Mrs. Mickey about the development of prehistoric hand tools from the Olduvai Gorge in Africa. Mr. Willis, who taught photography, helped me re-shoot photos from books to present as color slides for my project, and I delved into working in the darkroom. I was glad to be involved in schoolwork, to return to that world and keep myself from my preoccupation with Montana.

I was not allowed off campus for several weeks as part of my probation. Not that Troy, New York, was a big draw in 1973, but I missed walking to the little grocery store down the road and going with friends to the Army-Navy Surplus store downtown. I imagined myself like a nun, doing my duty to reach a goal; that made the restriction of movement somewhat more tolerable. After classes I walked three miles every day and used that time to sort a jumble of feelings, or mentally compose a next letter to Bill, or simply watch and listen to the atmosphere around campus.

As soon as I'd settled back at school, I sent a letter to Bill to explain what had happened. No doubt he was a little perplexed, since he couldn't even place me—why was I upending my life to find him? But he may also have been intrigued, or maybe even flattered. When he finally wrote back again in December, he was sympathetic to my attempt to be independent of a world I saw as profoundly distorted and troubled. At least he didn't regard me as foolish. "Don't give up your interest in the wild way," he wrote. "I found when I was your age, everyone was willing to give me advice against trying to find something they themselves never could hope to find. But the flame of an idea never could be put out, the dream drove me on and on to find that magic valley high in the Rockies where a cabin stood by a river, and the elk and deer and moose came to eat the hay I put out for them. And beautiful horses could take you to realms only eagles called their own. And each day was a beautiful gift that began with dawn, and ended with sleep, the joy of resting in peace and serenity, untouched by the sounds of the enemy of nature . . . MAN."

Through the rest of the school year, Bill and I exchanged letters. By June, I had assured him that I felt the same passion about living apart from a "broken" society, expressing my despair about our wastefulness, especially of energy, and environmental degradation. I praised him for his prowess at honing the skills he needed to live off the land and promised him that I was eager to learn those skills, too, and was capable of living a homesteader's life. I held back any misgivings about my ability to cope; the challenges of living without modern conveniences did not intimidate me as much as Bill's intolerance and disdain for anyone who was not as strong or as independent as he was, all of which shone through in his letters.

It was clear that Bill sought admiration. I understood that he was self-possessed but not gracious or humble in any way. These were qualities I'd been taught were essential to being a decent person—but I accepted that part of his character because we shared the all-important belief that we were living in a wasteful and greedy society. When he preached from his soapbox in his letters to me, I nodded my head, yes. And his poetic descriptions of his world and his experiences in the wilderness pulled me deep into that beauty.

Hollis had filled me in on a little of Bill's background after his visit to Val Halla the previous summer. When Bill was eighteen, he told me, he'd ventured from his home in Jacksonville, Florida, to Montana to work for a summer in the National Forest Service in Glacier Park. He was struck by the beauty of the vast wilderness and vowed to return, burying a ring and some other personal things in a special place. He had met a family near Hungry Horse and fallen for their thirteen-year-old daughter, Helen, and he promised himself that when he returned he would find her and take her with him to start his new life. And he did. Years later, after his service as a corpsman in the Navy in Vietnam, he came back to Montana, found Helen, retrieved his buried ring, and brought her north with him to the Canadian border to a homesteader's cabin with some supplies and lots of determination.

The cabin and land belonged to four men in the Flathead Valley who used it as a fishing camp. The property, about sixty acres, included a big barn, the homesteader's cabin (built around 1915), three or four one-room cabins along the river, and a larger cabin built by one of the property owners. The meadow had been cleared as a runway for small planes, and fishermen occasionally came there for a few days on the river. Helen's family had some connection to the property owners, and she and Bill were offered the homesteader's cabin if they would serve as caretakers. She stayed for four years, but by the time I met Bill in Denver, she'd been gone for a while. He never mentioned her in his letters.

For Christmas vacation I was back with family, with Denver friends, enjoying the life I intended to leave. It was bittersweet, and I felt a little blue thinking it would be my last Christmas at home. But I had not heard from Bill since our first exchange of letters, and I was looking forward to resuming our correspondence once I got back to school. A letter from him was waiting for me in my box, and I decided to share it with Mom and Dad as a way to include them in my thought process about living in Montana. I wanted my path to appear positive and certain.

Bill's second letter to me, dated Tuesday, December 24,

1973, was part admonition, part lesson, with a healthy dose of detail about his fantastic realm and his place within it.

Dear Ann,

Trying to remember that school for days, when on preparing to make a batch of bread this noon, your letter was under the flour can.

Was looking forward to meeting you, as I have great respect for people who choose the trail for adventure rather then sit at home idle watching others act in a blinking tube. It is a lesson to learn from, Ann. Never make a move in any direction unless you know all the problems beforehand . . . If there is one thing I can lay this wild existence I live to, it's using my eyes and ears to watch the ways of the world, then choose where my path should go. I haven't regretted a minute of it . . .

He went on to boast about his achievement in perfecting the brain-tanning method for buckskin. It was a special skill, and admirable; he was also far from humble about it. Still, I agreed entirely with his lecture about pursuing the most efficient use of motion or energy. Mom's influence served as a guidepost, and I felt pleased to concur with him on that front. I had expressed my concern to him about how waste and energy degraded the environment and we faced a grim future because of it and he agreed, confirming that this issue was not new and had been escalating for more than a century.

I figured out when a kid that something wouldn't last the way this country and the world wasted its earth's elements. That it was only a matter of time was simple to understand . . . and once I knew this, to choose a way of life that was proven by the Indians for thousands of years to be a good way was easy enough.

He pressed his philosophy, or what he called his "guiding principal for (the wilderness) life," which stressed becoming self-sufficient. He noted that he did have to buy certain supplies, like flour, salt, and beans, but that he needed very little else and didn't have to spend more than a few hundred dollars a year.

He closed the letter by reinforcing his reluctance to invite me to Val Halla: "Damn few people are invited to my door. Isolation is what I love, and I protect my privacy in every way I can. You would understand this once you lived it awhile, but to try and tell you is impossible."

Even though we were connecting on the most critical issues as far as I was concerned, he was not eager to yield or compromise his way of life. I had never been in a relationship, and couldn't understand how my presence would create such a huge shift for him. In my mind, I thought it was a simple matter: I would arrive at his cabin, and that would be that. I yearned for the simplicity of his lifestyle above everything else, and that singular, selfish focus blurred the reality of how my design might affect others.

In the next letter I sent to my parents, dated January 3, 1974, I was more insistent about my plan to join Bill after I finished school, claiming that he was a good friend and "almost mine," even mentioning that I loved him. That was the romantic part of my dream. But I also needed to substantiate my position that I felt "hypocritical" in the life I had grown up with, referring to our material wealth, and that I was "deprived of nothing, and not giving half enough," sharing my guilt of privilege and "selfishness." I conceded that "maybe the wild life is too rough for such a pampered untested girl—but if so—let me die among the deer and violent wildness of all nature. Perhaps this is close-minded but it is where I'm aiming and I refuse to be stopped."

Still, I wanted to assure my parents that I would always cherish the love of my family while I was "gone to the blood-red mountains," and I hoped that they would understand my hopes, fears, and desires. I closed the letter with, "Love to you both always with all my heart."

I felt passionate and determined, but it's hard to say why I thought of Bill as a friend after only two letters, or how I imagined that I loved him. The veneer of my delusions about the relationship could not hide the reality of this plan. My parents saw it as either ill-conceived or irrational (or both), and the drama and disdain in my letters home must have appalled them; Bill's voice was coming through mine. I was aware that I was being controversial, but I had to express conviction to emotionally shut out the world I would be leaving behind.

My parents shared their concerns when we talked weekly, urging me each time to consider carefully what I was putting myself up to. Did I understand the isolation and loneliness I would experience? What about the potential danger in wielding an axe, riding horses, firing a gun? Mom still worried about appendicitis and *What if?* They wanted to push me to visualize that lifestyle without the airbrush touch of romance in an edited storybook adventure. Yet in some small measure they accepted my desire to immerse myself in a wilderness experience, even though they were not comforted by the warnings and self-righteousness that filled Bill's letters.

Most Sundays I called my parents from the pay phone in the foyer downstairs around 5:00 p.m. Every call started the same way, with me saying hello and them answering from separate phones. "Hi Babes," my dad would say, then we'd generally follow what felt like a rehearsed script, except for a few details about school activities or notes about home life. The conversation always came around to my plan to live in Montana.

"Did you get my last letter?" I asked one Sunday. "Bill thinks I should go to the mountains!"

Mom tried to put a damper on my excitement. Her voice always started high, then dropped. "Babesy, you don't know this man, and you have *no* idea how to live in the wilderness."

Dad was more philosophical. "Now, Babes . . ." His voice started lower, then rose and fell gently from there. "I know you think this will be an exciting adventure, but you'll be throwing away your education and abandoning all of your potential if you sequester yourself in the mountains. We have worked hard to give you all you need to engage in this world, and you want to walk away from it. It's not too late to change your mind and consider applying to college."

"But Dad," I countered, "I will learn how to be self-sufficient, and I can still draw and paint up there, and it will be so beautiful . . ."

My urgency was not the right tool to convince them that I was thinking clearly. I didn't want to hurt them, and the only way I knew how to convince them what I was doing was right was to express my love for them. The idea that this alone might erase their concerns was, of course, entirely naive.

In the next letter I sent to my parents (dated January 27, 1974), I included both letters I'd received from Bill, hoping that they would be just as enthralled with the descriptions of his wilderness life as I was.

Dear Mom and Dad,

. . . Mountain Man wrote again—he more or less said he wanted company but that he's moving to B.C. Canada and he sent me a small piece of a tanned, smoked skin and oh oh oh I want to be up there a-tannin' hides too. [My hallmate's] dad says I should do what I think is right, long as I'm not hurting anyone—please tell me if . . . it is hurting you for me to want to do this O.K? I hope it's not, because I love you so much. I know you probably don't want me to go away so soon. Well, tell me what you think and be honest with me OK?

Annie

It was wishful thinking, and premature, to tell my parents that Bill wanted my company. In fact, there had been nothing like an invitation from Bill to live with him. Not yet. But I thought that if I was adamant, sounded sure-footed and ready, it would be just a matter of a few more letters before he accepted my plan to come to Montana as an "apprentice."

As a gesture of goodwill, I knit a scarf for Bill; it was a simple thing, but he appreciated it. In his letter dated February 7, when he addressed me as Annie instead of Ann, I was certain that he was warming up to me. After an opening lecture about his strengths and choices to live a life apart, he added, "When there are no teachers, there are few words for explanation. Talking to you has a strange effect on me, and things become clearer."

Did this mean he needed me as a sounding board? I was

pleased to be considered useful to him in any capacity. He thanked me for the scarf but didn't fail to add that it had taken me more time to knit it than it would take to sew a buckskin shirt together and reminded me about time allocation. Still, he did offer a friendly nod to my effort: "How many mountain men have a blue scarf to wear with their buckskins? Ha, I guess about 1 . . . I will wear it gladly."

The details in Bill's letters were intense and vivid, and I could easily imagine myself in the scene. Some of those musings were calm and creative, like quietly beading a piece of elk hide or watching the moose at the beaver ponds. He painted a detailed view of the beauty of his world for me:

> *A terrific storm blew in a foot of snow yesterday and last night, and now the sun is glorious and glittering. Blasts of wind are smashing the trees around the cabin, causing a cascading of hunks of snow, and showers of tiny white crystals, a million diamonds glinting in the light of afternoon sun . . . Across the river, the dark woods are suddenly whited out with a showering of snow from tree branches.*

Other depictions of his daily life were uncomfortable. In one letter he described the struggle to help Mia, his favorite old goat, as she birthed her three kids in the bitter cold. He tried to warm and nurse the kids, but none survived. I felt such sorrow thinking about how Mia must have been in pain with mastitis, and wondered who cared for the animals when Bill left to ride on his long treks. I imagined how I could be there to tend to the homestead while he took to the trail.

Mom and Dad were part of my journey and I considered them allies in my plans. But complete transparency about my fears and doubts would derail my forward momentum. I had to gently lead them so they wouldn't put a stop to it, or abandon me.

"Dear Mom and Dad," I wrote on February 10, "You have been great about this whole thing, and I really do appreciate your understanding and concern, thanks. Bill, I know, does not want to be tied up in any affair—he does not appreciate problems of anybody if they are imposing—you will think that he is not human, nor does he want people around—not so at all, he merely has escaped family ties and their problems and does not wish to retrace his footsteps."

Trying to cast him in a good light, I told them that he was beginning to trust me, and that he expressed his feelings openly and honestly, and that I hoped a bond was forming. I also wanted to keep my home life and my parents' everyday happenings within reach. "Write and tell me how the business is and family and you both and Josie (woof!). Love and kisses xox, Annie."

Winter midterms were coming up, and the snow and cold made it easier to do my homework curled up on the soft chairs in the library. Some girls seemed to always be there, draped over the chairs or leaning over their books at a table studying for a test or writing a paper. I saw them as role models, but they had good reason to study and do well, whereas I felt like my effort was unfocused, maybe even lost. Sitting and studying made me anxious and distracted; I much preferred doing something physical, like working on an art project or taking a walk. Mom and Dad's message about not living up to my potential was continually pushing to the front of my thoughts, and I fought with myself about the value of an education, given Bill's strident insistence that it was a waste of time. He warned me more than once that school was a "mockery to an education" and would "dull the mind."

Comments from a couple of my teachers on my midterm report card that semester confirmed that I was not doing as well as I could, and my parents were disappointed. I was unhappy with myself, too, since I knew I was capable of performing well academically.

The arts were easy for me, and I enjoyed the immersion and effort involved in producing a finished painting or poem. I loved my watercolor painting class with Mrs. Burdick. She brought in large sheets of rice paper one day and we set up on tables with blotter paper under the thin sheets to paint in a Japanese brush style. I worked from a photo of cherries on their branches and felt as though I was part of the swirl of water and line and color. Time disappeared and a painting emerged that did not seem to have come from me. She encouraged me to stay with botanical subjects, and subsequent paintings included a winter tree scene and a detailed drawing/painting of a long-leaved succulent plant, called Mother-in-law's Tongue, that lived in the studio.

Poetry class with Miss Prescott provided another outlet; there, my thoughts and emotions could merge within a framework of rhyme and meter and form. She assigned a different style of poem each week, and I loved piecing the words together like a puzzle. My dad's mother had been a stage actress and could recite many of Shakespeare's sonnets, so I felt a kinship with her through poetry.

On the weekends I would spend time with my friend Anne, who was incredibly artistic and always busy with her own projects. Anne seemed to embody an old soul and was the first person I knew to meditate. She didn't smoke or drink, and I liked that about her; I was in awe of her stability and creativity. She introduced me to the music of Odetta and Doc Watson on her stereo while we sat in her room and she worked on a crazy quilt. Her dorm had its own kitchen, and one day she decided that I needed to learn how to make apple pie. We peeled, cut, and piled the apples high under what baked into a flaky crust, and the smell of cooking apples permeated the whole dorm. It was an incredibly wonderful pie. My mom had never baked a pie that I could remember, so this felt like magic.

Other times, my friend Martha and I would hang out in her dorm room playing music. She could play guitar and had a great voice, clear and rich, somewhere in the realm of Joan Baez. Sometimes we went to the pottery studio to play with clay. On one of those outings I looked up from the coil bowl I was busy with to see Martha making a bong in the shape of a rooster. It had lots of character, and once it was fired, we had to try it out, so we snuck off campus to the cemetery across the road to smoke—something we did whenever we could. It was a stupid risk, but I assumed that we wouldn't get caught and we never did.

There were planned activities at school, and I looked forward to movie nights in the auditorium and dances with some of the boys' schools that were within a reasonable distance. Occasionally I would go down to one of the two living rooms, mostly to study or watch the nightly news with other schoolmates. One night a couple of girls brought their tape player in and blasted "I Heard It Through the Grapevine" by Marvin Gaye, and everybody in the room jumped up and joined in the line dance. That spontaneity provided the "drop everything" kind of fun that I knew was ephemeral and would probably not exist in my upcoming life with Bill.

Every Sunday evening Mrs. Carter hosted a tea in her

houseparent suite for the twelve of us on our dorm wing, and we all looked forward to her spread of homemade cookies and tea. School life was so civilized and secure, and I enjoyed being part of it, wanted to be involved, but I felt a little schizophrenic, as if I belonged to two worlds simultaneously.

When I talked to Mom and Dad on Sunday afternoons, I was glad to have something to share with them about my Emma Willard life so we didn't spend the whole time dwelling on the uncertainties of my future with Bill. They were generous to afford private school for me, and telling them about the details and enjoyment of our activities, or what I was doing in my classes, seemed like a way to show my appreciation.

CHAPTER FIVE

*B*y February, Bill was writing more often to share his stories—the door to join him was cracking open. He confided in me, or used the letters to sort his thoughts. Maybe, just maybe, I was becoming part of his life.

When he wrote to me on February 20, he was just back from Spokane, having driven all the way there because he had been invited by a Native American acquaintance to take part in an Indian artwork exposition.

It surprised me that he was willing to travel that distance in the middle of winter, except that he could only show off his brain-tanned buckskins, furs, beadwork, and engravings by entering the public realm. That engagement just confirmed his disdain for people, however, and gave him material for the negative views that he expressed in his letters. He didn't hold back. "I am just shortly returned from the squalor of a metropolis," he wrote, "and clearly the handwriting is on the wall . . . people are scared, worried, wondering what is going to happen . . ."

I wasn't sure what, exactly, he was referring to, but I figured it had something to do with the state of the world. He continued:

I had hoped I was wrong, that some powerful leader would arise, and change the course of this unseeing blindness that has gripped the world. But, the only sound over there in the big city was

*the S sign with twin slash marks II or $HELL THE DOLLAR
SIGN. Just like the boys in Vietnam who all said "It will never
happen to me" thousands of them were snuffed out, more maimed
and torn inside out. So it is with this glorious system of ours, nobody
can grasp the simple fact that the 1st 100,000 years did not use a
millionth of the world's resources compared to the last 100 years.
Nobody can grasp the fact that a simple culture existed in perfect
harmony with nature unchanged all those 1st 100,000 yrs while
what can best describe the culture of the last 100 other then 'THE
MECHANICAL CULTURE.'*

Okay, I thought. He summed up what I also believed
about our wasteful ways with a simple, numerical phrase.
But he went on with something that sounded a little off,
like a conspiracy theory:

*The drug scene is part of a master plan, Annie, to control
men's minds. So long as kids can get it, so long as it holds its illegal
status it has a million times the attraction force because of the law-
breaking challenge, they will be satisfied with whatever the system
of laws try to pull off. In other words, the system wants no one to
question them, as Nixon has so brilliantly proved. He has gotten
away with every underhanded ploy there is, yet no one can stand up
to him.*

*. . . Easier to sit back an' puff fake dreams then try to be strong
enough to live them. You haven't said, and I hope you aren't in it. I
chose to alienate myself at 14 from a self-defeating culture . . . what
willpower it takes to stand alone and a part of what you're
supposed to be.*

Was he referring to the peace protesters, or hippie culture in general? I was allied in support of both, and felt that the pushback against Nixon was a positive attempt to change the culture of war and white supremacy. But I did not try to unfold my views on this with Bill, since I knew that would end the relationship. It was strategic on my part, but I had to convince him that my goal was clear.

When I wrote to Bill, I shared my opinions and concerns that mirrored his views. My sole intent was to show him that I would be an asset and not an invader in his life. It made me uneasy that I was involved in the pot smoking culture that Bill was condemning, and I was well aware that I had given in to the allure and habit. I wanted to be stronger than that, and overcome my weakness; once I was in Montana, I would have to leave that part of my life behind.

Mom and Dad had given up trying to convince me not to go to Montana. It didn't lessen their concern, but they handed over the responsibility of my future to me, which was a little surprising and scary. I was in charge and there was no reverse gear. I had to assume a position of self-reliance and strength, even though I didn't feel it most days.

That winter, Mom penned a letter to Bill:

Dear Mr. Atkinson,

As you undoubtedly know, our daughter Annie is completely captivated by your way of life—or at least the idea of it, as she has never experienced wilderness and survival as you know it. As you also may know she left school late in October bent on finding you near Polebridge. We were able to reach her by telephone in Great Falls and she willingly came home to discuss the matter not only with us, but also with the principal of her school who happened to be in Denver at that time. It was a highly irregular action on her part & also the parts of her friends who not only encouraged her to leave school but supplied her with the necessary cash for her airline ticket. The school was extremely open-minded in accepting her back with a most lenient probation.

Annie is still determined to experience your kind of existence and is now hoping to join you in the Spring as part of an independent study program, which, apparently the school has given her permission to do. Mr. Chappell & I are overwhelmed & confused by this whole concept; needless to say it is not the kind of action that parents can easily condone, especially knowing so very little about you & your intentions as far as Annie is concerned.

We know that Annie feels very deeply that she must try the wilderness & she seems to think that you are the only person who could teach her. Understandably the pressures of certain aspects of civilization are great on today's youth and certain values must be questioned. Thus Mr. Chappell and I cannot deny Annie the right to explore & expose herself to the values other than she has known. Annie is only 17 and in many ways immature. She is appealing and attractive though she has never had a beau.

This was where the letter ended. Mom was feeling helpless and had wanted to contact Bill since she and Dad were part of the equation, and she thought she should share their concerns with him. She never sent the letter, however.

I never discussed my parents in my letters to Bill, and he never asked about them.

By now, Bill was starting to accept the notion that I might join him. Over and over he presented the challenges I would face, including his intolerance for anyone who did not meet his standards. Somehow I had convinced him that I was serious and certain that I would not be a burden in his life, and that I'd be able to take on all the trials he warned me about.

In a letter to me, postmarked March 8, he opened with descriptions of the drifting snow, the smell of the wood smoke snaking into the sky, and the beauty of silence. And then he offered a cautious invitation into his world:

. . . So, you see, the realm of the silent man beside the river is vast. Mountain valleys reach their fingers up the creek toward the divide on either side of the river that runs before him. That it takes strenuous effort to wander into those forbidden realms you understand . . . I tell you all this in strictest confidence, for there must be understanding of basics first. Since that time sequence would be rather abrupt if you arrive, patience would wear thin swiftly if you allow preconceptions of the wrong nature to cloud the atmosphere. One thing I know, I have no desire to waste time and energy. . . . Life is too real and sweet . . . alone . . . to begin the sparring of give an take with anyone, in this world of mine. Total independance in this life should be your first and foremost goal, and remain so. Any chore, any job, any necessity automatically is done . . . after once learned. You best understand your a slave . . . until such a time when you suddenly realize when you sit beside the river you are a master of a world of wild savagery and beauty shared only with eagles and the wolf, the lion and griz, the wolverine and water wolf . . . and that is the finest gift there is.

He closed simply, and included the following set of tenets:

POSITIVE ASSUMPTIONS FOR FUTURE PROJECTIONS FOR SURVIVAL OF THE FITTEST

1st premise: HISTORY DECREES IN THE EVOLUTION OF MAN EACH INNOVATION IN WEAPONRY MUST BE USED TO ITS ULTIMATE POINT UNTIL REPLACED BY A NEWER INNOVATION. (THAT INEXORABLE POINT IN TIME WILL CAUSE THE EXPONENTIAL RISE OF CIVILIZATION TO DROP ABRUPTLY BACK TO A NEAR NEOLOTHIC PERIOD.)

2nd premise: ALL MEN ARE BORN TO DIE.

3rd premise: ALL MEN ARE SOCIALLY ORIENTED ON GROUNDS OF SHEER NUMERICAL NECESSITY.

4th premise: THE COLLEGE DEGREE IS A SUBLIMINAL DECEPTION & MOCKERY TO AN EDUCATION.

5th premise: THE CULTURE OF THE EARTH'S 1ST 100,000 YRS. UTILIZED 1/1000th OF THE EARTH'S ELEMENTAL RESOURCES COMPARED TO THE LAST 100 YEAR CULTURE. (YET THE 1ST SYSTEM WAS DESTROYED IN APPROX. 30 YRS IN THE UNITED STATES.)

6th premise: THE EXPONENTIAL PROJECTION FOR AN ADDITIONAL 50 YRS AT CURRENT RATES OF ELEMENTAL USAGE INCREASE IS UNFEASIBLE.

7th premise: WORLD FOOD PRODUCTION IS EXPONENTIALLY DECREASING TO POPULATION INCREASE (INFLATION ON SIMPLE NECESSITIES IS RISING BEYOND CONTROL.)

8th premise: AN EXPONENTIAL PROJECTION FOR
WORLD PEACE FOR HUMANITIE'S SAKE FOR THE
NEXT 10 YEAR PERIOD IS UNTENABLE.

9th premise: THE HUMAN EQUATION IS PRESENTLY
SCHEDULED TO SELF DESTRUCT . . .

10th premise: THE MAN WHO LIVES IN TOTAL
IGNORANCE OF ALL THE WORLD BEYOND HIS
IMMEDIATE ENVIRONMENT LIVES A HAPPIER MORE
CONTENTED LIFE IN A FREEDOM UNKNOWN TO
THOSE WHO TRY TO SWALLOW ALL OR PART OF
HUMANITY.

11th premise: THE 11TH HOUR WILL BE LEFT TO
THOSE WHO LEARN TO EXIST IN COMPATIBLE
HARMONY WITH A SELF-PERPETUATING
ENVIRONMENT.

Yes, I thought, reading his premises, *that looks about
right.* It was hard to disagree with most of what he put forward, except maybe the college degree as a mockery to education. That was his particular spin, and I was not entirely
convinced that education was such a bad thing.

His repeated self-aggrandizement and diatribe against
"the system" put me off, and I did not always sympathize or
agree with him, but I wagered that he had a softer side that
I could appeal to and trusted that I could find a way to negotiate that part of his character once we were together.
The fierceness of his demands made me nervous, but I understood that it was his way of protecting his world from
the outside and that he wanted to make sure that I knew
what I would have to do to earn my keep.

In my world of civility and refinement, his temperament
would not have been tolerated; I had never met anyone who

had so completely renounced American culture and built a life apart. When Bill wrote about my role as a "slave" until I mastered a level of independence in the life he lived, I believed he was referring to the difficulty of learning how to survive in a wilderness environment, not addressing my relationship with him. But there *was* an inevitable role I would have to play; it made sense to me that if he was my teacher I would serve him in exchange for his teaching, resources, and sacrifice of time. I imagined myself as an apprentice and thought he would grow fond of me—like a younger sister or maybe, eventually, an equal partner. Somewhere along the way I hoped to become the woman I thought Bill would accept. So, as Bill grew more receptive to my plan to join him, I felt relieved.

In a February correspondence, Bill asked me to send a photo of myself. For communications class we were issued simple cameras and taught how to process the black-and-white negatives and make prints. My friend Jackie took some pictures of me outside and we ran down to the darkroom to develop a contact sheet of negative-size photos. We didn't make full-size prints that day, so I sent Bill a couple of the inch-square photos to give him a notion of how I looked.

When he wrote back on March 8, he opened with a cranky accusation that I was being rude to send such a tiny image. I immediately responded with a note that I felt was apologetic but also firm enough to show that I had some backbone. I wanted him to appreciate that I could hold my own, even in this small episode, so I told him that I was plenty sturdy and looks shouldn't matter, since it was my conviction that was more important.

In his next letter, dated March 18, he conceded, "You're a firebrand to think and talk like that, and you know it.

And your [sic] damn proud of it, and I'm damn proud of you for it . . . as you see . . . I did so enjoy your letter, I wanted nothing more than to see what kind of fire you would answer that letter last . . . but too, I wanted to see you, really see you when I asked for a pic. Can you begrudge me that?"

In that same letter in which I'd defended myself about the photos, I'd included my own version of a fierce rant about the state of the world and my need to walk away from it. We were in the middle of an intense conversation on paper that was both compelling and intimidating, but it felt honest and tangible, and from the safety and comfort of my dorm room, I was drawn into his world. He continued to warn me at every turn of what was ahead if I joined him, even as he acknowledged that I was falling in line with the strong will to pursue that life.

"All you say of the Great White Way is too true," he wrote in one letter. "Amazed that you so well know it at your age . . . But the world of the silences is not easily grasped in a few lessons . . . I can well understand you want it. I can well understand why. But I can also foresee the problems of sharing it with you, for even a while. First, have you never lived where all time is free, for you to decide any and everything to do with it?"

He boasted that he did not have any use for a clock, which imposed a "regulation" on his time, and he questioned my ability to govern my own time. These were the same words of caution about the potential for loneliness or despair that my parents, headmaster, and others had pressed. I wasn't worried about it, however; I was much more concerned about my ability to do the physical work, not making mistakes, and the trial of a long, cold winter.

I persisted in my soft push to enter his world, and in that same letter from Bill, dated March 18, he finally, cautiously, opened the door. The invitation came with a list of caveats—most importantly, that he would not cater to a "willful" woman who would disturb his lifestyle with demands or criticism. "I cannot compromise, cannot change, cannot accept anything less than that which I know is real and beautiful," he wrote. "Offers I have refused because I knew the process of pre-programming was too well advanced, the willful right of a white woman too long ingrained to ever accept the simple life and contribute to its perfection . . ."

Again, he put down the weakness that he saw as endemic to white culture and tentatively endorsed my desire to walk away from it: "Annie, you mention escaping being labelled what seeking this existence is called . . . I'm aware I represent something unknown in this age of blindness. The reality I live is too real, too harsh at times, too violent, and yet there are the tender times, the gentle times too of beauty, and love shared . . . I know the finest life to live is a shared one . . . but the chance to find it again is rather rare. We will have to meet and see. I cannot discourage your desire to escape nor the idea of coming to Val Halla. Somehow the Above Ones mean for certain things to happen. If so, we will soon know. To deny this is impossible."

He followed with the prescription of exercise to gain the physical strength and skill I would need, including the ability to "ride a horse bareback at breakneck speed," throw a tomahawk, and "gut a rabbit in a few minutes' time." Also, "kill with a rifle." Well, I had been on dude ranch horses, going at a walk, and I had shot my grandfather's Remington .22 rifle—but only at targets, never to kill anything. As for a tomahawk—I would just have to learn how to throw one when I got there. (*But what*, I wondered, *do you kill with a tomahawk?*)

At the end of his letter from March 18, Bill recommended that I look at the drawings and paintings representing Native Americans and the early frontiersmen in the mid-1800s in *The West of Alfred Jacob Miller*, by Marvin C. Ross, and ended with a quote from the author and poet Robert Service:

> . . . *Only the few who drink the wind can the reason for his life be known.*
>
> *It is a life that must be left to only the FEW WHO WALK ALONE.*
>
> *You know he's one who walks alone It takes a special kind of breed to throw the CHAINS of those back home And choose to live by simple needs.*
>
> *Another chunk thrown on the coals send flickers cross my new friend's face*
>
> *Tis plain to see the peace he knows he's the sole member of his own race.*
>
> *The feeling of just being there in all that*
>
> *mountain wilderness*
>
> *ALONE AND WILD AND FREE,*
>
> *No cares to weigh the mind,*
>
> *WHY LESS?*

Bill knew very little about me, of course, and I did not dare mention my confusion and struggle with sex abuse, pot smoking, alcohol, and the upper-crust world to which I belonged. I didn't have the perspective or maturity to link my distorted relationship with my brother-in-law to my upcoming adventure and attraction to a man I barely knew.

Life in Montana was alluring for what it represented as a lifestyle and ethic, but I also thought that it would fix everything in my life that I could not control, including the possibility of failure in a world that seemed to measure success by your social status and income.

My friends and classmates had aspirations to become doctors or professional artists, or to take on larger social problems and fix them, and I admired them, but I could not picture how any of that might happen, and I was afraid of the hard work involved in even trying. That was the simplified version of my options as I saw them, and I had run those conceptual loops through my mind often enough that they'd become a sort of reality of the future that I sorted into two categories: one that I would fit into, and one that I wouldn't.

It was a fight-or-flight response to my situation, and I was not introspective enough to try to clean up my mess from the inside out.

CHAPTER SIX

*B*ill's forceful commentary about the threat of an apoc‐
alyptic future solidified my fears, and gave me the
justification I needed for stepping out of my current world.
His prediction about impending food shortages due to over‐
population and exploitation and destruction of resources
matched my views entirely. Failure of leadership was part
of the mix, as was the ugliness that humans exhibit when
their access to food, water, and a livelihood are threatened.
In a letter sent on March 24, Bill pressed the urgency I also
felt. "Now, time is running out," he wrote. "The culture of
the mechanical society is doomed to self-destruct. I've
known it for eight years, and can even fairly guess how long
it has to run. . . . I'm no prophet of doom, just plain common
sense and a few facts that can't be disputed would give
anyone the similar answer . . ."

Again, he questioned my reason for staying in school,
even though in a previous letter I'd told him that although I
was perfectly capable of coping in society, I was ready to
walk away. He appreciated my position but warned, "It is a
deadly game of roulette you wish to play coming here . . .
Once you get a taste of the feeling of freedom far from the
frothing fool's world of bull feces, there is no place to go
back to. None, Annie. You're a race apart, and to have to
cope once again is not even questionable. It just isn't possi‐
ble."

He continued, "I like your fire, Annie . . . but it takes a powerful physical person both in body and mind to walk where machines cannot reach." Referring to "the hardships, the hours, the time, the beauty, the rain, the snow, the mud, the physical torcher of climbing high steep trails over passes," he insisted I not waste any time regarding training for strength and endurance. I would have to be able to manage from the first day, because "there won't be time to break in a city girl."

He realized that I had a brain and he approved in a weird, almost condescending way. "The mind seems to be damn sharp . . . a good indication, for nothing is worse then dull mediocrity. Believe me, girl, you're biting off quite a chunk seeking what you think. To go against everything you're raised to believe . . . and finding it . . . that is a monumental task so few ever challenge themselves anymore. I have to admire you for it." And yet, he wrote, "from your world I expect no intrusions, and will tolerate none, my own people wish to come up and visit me, but they only bring their twisted worn out ideals, and warped religion. My tolerance level isn't the warmest to such people [who] say of me that I'm right arrogant when I wear the lion skin cape around my shoulders. You bet I am . . ."

Yes, I could see that. He finished:

Hell, I'm rambl'n on. Belly full of elk steak, fire at my back, chicks just began laying and the goat is about to kid which means fresh milk again. The horses are fat and eager, and the cats sleeping peaceful. What a world to contemplate walking away from.

Of your world, I call them the walking dead, sightless to the world of natural reality, blind to their own bigotry, apathetic to their illusions, senseless in a blind faith to a religion of mockery of

man . . . I bet you'd make a hit presenting my 11 premises before your
English or History class.
—Bill

Well, I was signed up. And I was a little intimidated, because he was outwardly so fierce, but I believed that his experience in Vietnam justified his need to escape, and to protect himself. The war had partly shaped Bill's response to the world; how could it not? He occasionally described the scene in Da Nang, where he had been stationed for his overseas tour as a corpsman for the Navy from 1965 to 1967. He built his own hooch, or bunk space, apart from the rest of his troop and refused to wear regulation clothing. His officers were opposed to his independence, but he defiantly wore his own boots, belt, and his own knife from home. Because he could handle the trials of wartime medical service, and never touched drugs or alcohol, his peers left him alone. On his twenty-third birthday, in 1965, he ran twenty miles on Red Beach, a half-mile-long stretch on Da Nang harbor, back and forth. His self-discipline must have been intimidating to his mates and superiors, for they did not treat him with respect for his strength but, out of their own weakness, with disdain. At least, that was how Bill told it.

Current affairs played into everyone's reality, and the social malaise about our involvement in the Vietnam War was tangible. I'd first heard about the war as an eight- or nine-year-old, in 1965. The details were not important to me then, but when my brothers, cousins, and friends faced the draft, I instinctively resented and feared it. My oldest brother, Dos, had enlisted in officer training school to avoid the draft and served as an officer in the Air Force in Oxnard, California, where he found a way around regular military life to enjoy sea kayaking and bowling and do a little desk work. A few years after that, in 1969, my other brother, Geof, was ready to head for Canada if his draft number came up. That was a sore point with my dad, especially since they were already at odds about Geof's attitude of rebellion and criticism of the high-society culture we'd grown up in. Dad had served as a lieutenant in World War II, and had been stationed for a time in the Azores. He'd never seen combat, but he'd believed, along with the rest of the nation, that our country was fighting that war for all the right reasons. I am not sure where he stood on Vietnam, but no doubt he thought my brother was shirking his national duty.

It was a warm, bright day when the two of them had an argument that ended in a fistfight in the front yard, and my heart almost shattered. I rushed out to try to break them up, but one of them snapped at me to go inside. Mom was shaken too. Their anger had never erupted to a physical level before, and I both feared and respected their passion in fighting for what they believed in. I figured that I would have gone to Canada, too, if I had been faced with that decision.

The war was ever-present, year after year, on the nightly news, and it was grim. The protests and love fests that erupted and bloomed in the late 1960s seemed like the right response, although most of my understanding about the war came from my peers, and from older friends and siblings we knew. In our need to find our young voices, we listened to the music of protest and felt the empowerment of the messages of righteous anger and prayers for peace, and we envisioned a different way. We hoped and believed these efforts would move the needle in the right direction. In our sophomore Communications class, we studied current events, and when our teacher brought in the photos of the Mi Lai massacre one day, we expressed our collective anguish.

Some of my Emma Willard classmates were amazingly well-versed about the logistics, history, and horrors of the war in Vietnam. On a winter evening of my junior year in 1973, in our dorm living room, one of our classmates gave a full seminar on the history of our involvement in Vietnam, complete with maps and diagrams, just out of the need to share the terrible truth. That Spring, Jane Fonda, an Emma Willard alumna from the class of 1955, came to share her experience, anger, and fears related to the Vietnam War. Her tangible emotions brought the horror home for me in a way that I hadn't known before. In my mind the war was a nebulous cloud of dark political dealings, chemical poisons, guerilla activism, burning monks, and traumatized vets.

For our sonnet assignment in Miss Prescott's poetry class that winter, I found a way to share my sarcastic and uncomfortable feelings about the politics of war:

The President has sought an end to war.
A fine and dandy thing that he has done!
If bombing ceased it would be si un (such a) bore,
To watch the news would simply be no fun.
No mines to blow the farmers off the land,
Which they so protectively defend.
With America the Brave to lend a hand,
You'd think the North would never dare to send
A tank, or plane (which we Americans
most likely sent, an act of foreign aid)
Southward, where mighty stand Republicans!

When you and I were young, I'm sure we played
A type of game with guns; and yes,
You could agree that we have made a mess.

✕

CHAPTER SEVEN

*S*chool was the backdrop for my life. Winter was disap-
pearing, and while my classmates were waiting to
hear from colleges about acceptance, I was getting ready for
my life in the mountains. I had started running at least two
miles each day and could manage a score of pushups, challenged myself to swim a mile in the small pool in the basement of the chapel, and was working to build endurance
and muscle whenever I had an opportunity. Would it be
enough? I wasn't sure I'd ever be up to the levels of strength
and independence Bill insisted I have, but I had some confidence that I could gain even more strength once I was
there. At just over one hundred pounds and standing five
foot four, I appeared more capable of dusting and sewing
than lifting bales of hay and scraping deer hides. But I had
always considered myself tough, a tomboy, and could overcome any size drawbacks with fierce determination and wit.

By April, the continuing conversation with Mom and
Dad to prove that my plan was taking shape was exhausting all of us. Wanting to show them how deeply I cared for
them, and hoping to apply a salve on their aching hearts, I
wrote a poem for them.

Dear Mom and Dad,

So too, am I torn inside, but yes, I must go—despite dangers—don't we all face certain dangers always? The half-poem has some thoughts in response, maybe in a plea, and also in thanks for your blessings. I know it's especially hard for you to let go your youngest, and I've had qualms about leaving home too, but even so, it won't be for always.

I am growing stronger running, and I know that I can handle a fair amount of wear and tear. And I'll go up there protected so that I won't get pregnant—that's the last thing I'd want right away. Yet I'm very excited (along with a tiny bit of fear) and it certainly will be good for me, maybe I'll learn at least how to cook a stew. Anyway, you've been so good to me there is nothing I can say to tell you how much I really do love you both, always, so deep in my soul, and that love is just now showing its face, for it comes from the deepest places of my heart. And I know that we are one.

Annie

When the wind beckons so soft will you turn away,
knowing it calls but once?

When such cry for a free spirit wells inside your soul,
can your heart still beg you to ignore?

No, ever my soul has pleaded a freedom.

Now, though it has been contained, it stretches beyond the grasp of reason, conscience it now obeys, simplicity it craves.

As an eagle soars, so too does my spirit—it encircles the yet icy snow-capped mountains far above a newly green field—so must I not follow it for sake of sanity, or must body and soul exist one without the other?

Two loves, one the earth, where I have grown, tended with gentle
care, one the sky, new and where I will catch the wind, granted
wings to fly, perhaps to fall; yet if I fall, will not Mother
Earth always be below me?

Who can say where my wings will carry? Although I must fly,
Never will I mistake or misplace your love for me, nor must you
forget how strong my love flows to you.

My conviction was not enough to convince my parents
that I would be fine in Montana. Mom and Dad needed
some consolation and confirmation about my choice and
invited Tom and Diane Carson over to find out more about
Bill, and how they felt about the situation. Diane agreed
that Bill was fiercely independent, but she assured them
that he was not a brute and would take care of me. She
managed to allay some of their fears. Tom Carson, meanwhile, appreciated Bill for his carefully drawn scrimshaw
etchings of predators and Indian Chieftains, his care in
learning the brain-tanning skills of the Native Americans,
and the beautifully detailed beadwork on his buckskin
shirts. Their friend and artist who was represented at the
gallery, Hollis Williford, had gone to Montana to visit Bill,
and that spoke volumes, since Hollis was such a gentleman
and would not tolerate a less-than-quality character. Diane
was honest, caring, and accepting of others; I loved and
admired her, and trusted her more as a mentor and friend
than as a parent figure. She was sure of my ability, and
solidly supportive.

April 22, 1974

Dear Annie Babe,

A few weeks ago your Mom and Dad asked us to stop by for a drink to talk about your venture planned for this summer. It was apparent without being terribly perceptive, that they were hoping we had some magical solutions for getting you to stay home and think more provincial thoughts! We talked a lot about Bill, and made it very plain that we hold a lot of admiration and respect for him; that we felt although he would be a strenuous companion for you and would work the hell out of you, we feel he will take good care of you. Besides, I know you are smart enough to know the way out of there if things get crumby.

Well, I have stalled a lot, because I was filled with a feeling that any letter I would write to you (which was sort of their request) would be a dreadful disappointment to them. You see I have really tried hard to project Cini into your position and have tried like hell to see if I would feel differently were it she who was in love with the idea of Mountain Man. It's a weird mental picture, because I don't ever think of Cini as putting out that kind of physical WORK for anyone, and I suspicion the only thing they would have in common is his piano.

But the only conclusion I can come to is that if you were mine, I'd have to let you go. You are so determined, and seem to know— not think—that it is what you want to do . . . so with all my heart I'd have to say make it a good experience, cuz it's sure one to tell your grandchildren! If you were mine, I'd want to hear from you cuz I'd be scared for you, so take a stack of postcards all addressed and stamped like I send to camp with Danny (haha) or better yet set up a time every day to keep a diary-type account of the things you do and mail it off now and then. Your folks can save them for you so that you can publish them someday!!!!!

Well, this very morning your Mom called to say things were cool; she'd had a super letter from you and that is so great, because this is a very difficult thing for them to let you do. They feel a sense of failure on their own part, and as I say scared for you. But I know that will disappear if it turns out to be an enriching and rewarding experience, and they know you are O.K. Anyway, now I don't seem to have any problem writing to you and I'm very glad for that.

You are a little bit mine . . . and I love you.

Diane

p.s. Hope you don't mind your folks sharing Bill's letters with us. D.

In a last letter home before graduation in June, dated May 2, I wanted a peaceful close to what had been such a turbulent and trying time for my parents, and for me. This last letter was in response to one Dad had written to express his fears about my journey, but also his trust that I would use my best judgment, work to better myself, and use my skills and education to share with others in a broader context someday.

"Spring here too is refreshing, after seeing blank grey walls staring, the ivy is so beautiful," I wrote. "Dad, your letter was so honest and understanding—I can't even tell you how good it was for both of us that you said that . . . Now it's five weeks until June 9, and the thing that I'm anxious about is 3 term papers—hope to do one this weekend."

I added a little description about finding a broken bowl in an old dump while I was with Martha, just to share something of my school life. Then I confirmed that Bill had invited me to come to Val Halla, but there would be a trial period, explaining, "he makes it clear that for a while I will be invading his territory and how hard the work is. I would be stupid to think that all will go smoothly always—I'm scared, but that will make me all the more cautious and ready to exert myself. Really I can't wait at all—this is something so few ever try and I can't even tell you how much this means to me." I promised to take the advice from Diane Carson to send lots of postcards and letters home while I was with Bill, "which for sure I'll do—I wouldn't leave you out of my experiences and life for anything. Glad you're swimming—I swim a half mile, run 2 and can do 32 pushups fairly well now. It's only a beginning . . . Love you so much—take good care, xoxo Annie."

✗

CHAPTER EIGHT

*G*raduation day finally arrived. School was behind me and within a few weeks I would leave home and head north to live with Bill in Montana. Mom and Dad and my mother's parents had traveled from Denver to be with me. I felt honored and relieved to have their support, especially since Manna and Pappy didn't very often take part in their grandchildren's activities outside of our routine family get-togethers. For a graduation gift they gave me a book of beautiful wilderness photographs of the High West. Pappy was eighty-seven but still going strong, and it amazed me that they were still traveling and so active at their age, considering that my grandmother was suffering from arteriosclerosis. Pappy, especially, made it a point to enjoy life.

I was not about to buy a new dress, because that would put me in the category of "consumer" and it seemed wasteful for a one-time event, so I borrowed my aunt's graduation dress from the '40s, since it represented something familiar about the past.

Agnes DeMille, a renowned dancer and choreographer throughout her long life, spoke at our commencement. No doubt she gave us sage advice about doing well by doing good, drawing on our strengths, and becoming women with something to add to the world. Mom and Dad especially enjoyed her speech, but I would remember little about it.

My goodbyes with friends were brief. There were a few hugs, some tears, and a couple of last looks at the places on campus that had become special for me: the tower, and the huge oak that Martha and I had often climbed. I had insisted that my yearbook picture include that tree.

Before we returned home to Colorado, my parents and I drove to Connecticut to visit my dad's only sibling, Joan. She was four years younger than Dad and in her second marriage with my uncle Cuz. Joan had raised seven children, even though she had virtually no use of her arms since she had contracted polio in 1946 after the birth of her first daughter. But she could drive a car adapted for her feet (way too fast for winding New England roads) and all of the counters in the house were low so she could do some cooking or pour a drink. She and Cuz, with their three daughters from that marriage and their adopted son, were headed for southern Spain, where they had recently built a house on a hillside that looked over the coast of the Mediterranean and Gibraltar. They encouraged me to join them—maybe a last-ditch effort in cahoots with my parents to try to redirect my plans. Any other time, I would have jumped at the chance to go, but I merely thanked them and told them that my plan for Montana was all set.

Once we were home, Mom helped me make a list and get everything ready for Montana. Cowboy boots and leather work gloves were high on my list, while Mom's priorities were birth control and first aid; together, we were balanced in our collaboration. She was with me for my first gynecological exam, so I could get the Pill. Dr. Blanchette was Mom's gynecologist and had attended my birth, although he just missed my arrival, so it was like closing a loop seeing him. Mom took me shopping for cowboy boots at Shepler's Western Wear store in downtown Denver. I thought they would be good work boots, since cowboys wore them, but I was not entirely sure I liked them: they pinched my toes and the hard leather soles felt slippery on the shoe department floor. For cooler days, I picked out a navy blue wool jacket with snaps.

I had learned that a friend of a friend was driving to Kalispell, at the north end of Flathead Lake, to see her mother at the end of June and could take me at least that far. Sarah was not much older than I was, had red hair, and struck me as daring and feminine. Standing in the early light with my army duffel and daypack (and Teddy tucked away), I hugged Mom and Dad one last time when she pulled into the drive to pick me up. The moment was full to overflowing with anticipation about the journey, and the tears that come with deep goodbyes. I felt enormously grateful to be going with my parents' blessing; nothing would have felt right without that. Still, this was a departure with my parents that all of a sudden felt too permanent. There wasn't a checklist in my head of what I was leaving behind, and why, but those uncomfortable places were not far below the surface, and leaving home was sorrowful and scary, like stepping into dark water with undercurrents.

I promised I would write. As we pulled away, I waved goodbye and quietly wiped my tears.

The drive north from Denver to Kalispell is a thousand miles, and we drove straight through. Wyoming rolled by in a roan-colored blur and I dozed after dark since I was not driving.

We arrived in Kalispell early in the morning and spent

a day at Sarah's mother's house. The next morning, she and a friend drove me up to the border where Bill lived.

The route was beautiful; small farms and occasional trailer homes and roadside bars in the lake valley gave way to more densely forested terrain as we headed up the North Fork of the Flathead River. The dirt road followed along above the river, at times with a steep drop down that made me a little edgy, especially when we met any of the logging trucks that seemed to rule the back roads.

Across the river valley toward the east, the jagged peaks of Glacier Park rose 10,000 feet to cut into the sky. We stopped at the Polebridge store and post office, about sixty miles north of Kalispell, to take a break and quietly check it out. There were a few shelves stocked with canned goods and boxes of pasta and the usual small assortment of sundries, candy, ammunition, fishing bait and lures, and a paltry supply of fruit and vegetables. The sales counter doubled as the post office, and there was a pay phone hung on a post in the middle of the room.

The next twenty-three miles of dirt road seemed both eternal and much too short—the last leg of my long journey to reach Bill at his Val Halla. I tried to etch that part of the road into my brain: my new world.

Sarah dropped me off across from the road that led into the property where Bill lived. She and her friend wished me luck, and the clunk of the car door closing had an unsettling sound of finality. She turned around and they drove off.

I stood for a minute, just to gather myself and untie the knot in my stomach. The Canadian border crossing was right there, with a small cabin for the border guard, but the bridge was out from a flood the year prior so there was no access to Canada. The crossing still had to be attended, though, and the border guard and his wife may have noticed my arrival that day; I did think I saw the window curtain on the door drop back into place as I stood there taking in my surroundings. Before I picked up my duffel bag, I took a few steps off the road and into the trees to pee, since I did not need that pressure when I met Bill.

Finally, after a year of imagining it, I had made it to this place Bill called Val Halla—his paradise in the wilderness, his cabin in Montana. It was the last day of June 1974. Lugging my bulky duffel bag, I walked about a quarter of a mile along a road to the cabin, the river running parallel beyond some tall pines to my left. There were the three or four one-room fishing cabins I had seen in Hollis's slides a year earlier. Ahead of me was the barn and Bill's well-worn red Ford truck. The pungent, sweet tang of newly mown fields filled my head as the meadow opened ahead of me, stretching for a half mile along the river.

I'd thought Bill would be outside, but he wasn't, so I felt more as if I were encroaching than arriving. He hadn't known exactly when to expect me. When I got to the cabin I hesitated a moment, then knocked. Those few seconds at the door were the space between childhood and adulthood, and I sensed that my path from that time forward would be forever determined by this place, this man.

Bill opened the door and stepped toward me, and we shook hands. At six feet tall he filled the doorway, and between the height, his long hair—held in place with a beaded headband—and full beard, he was an imposing figure. He sized me up quickly; I could tell he was examining this new element in his life. He was not cold, but neither was he openly welcoming. He'd warned me that he guarded his world intensely, and it was this guardedness that greeted me.

Having done his time as a corpsman in the Navy, Bill

had experienced some of the worst of what a war can expose, and his outer shell was tough. He was only thirty-three but his demeanor was outwardly bold and gruff, like that of an older man who'd seen hardship. But he had found his way back to a part of the world that he could tolerate. Both of us were sure in our own way that a life apart from society was healthier and more positive, although our paths and experiences were separated by our age and upbringing. I had just dropped myself into his life, abandoning what I had come from—boarding school, Denver society, the movement toward college—and was now standing in a world I passionately wanted to embrace.

If I could prove myself tough enough to handle the work and isolation, life would be simple and peaceful, and there was a chance Bill would grow fond of me. Maybe it would be escape, or maybe freedom; I just knew I needed to feel strong and healthy. This rugged life I'd landed myself in would push me in that direction, and I thought that every challenge would be another step toward independence and happiness.

That day would be a true test, the first in a long string of first experiences. What I did not yet understand was how to judge my own ability, or the risks involved in my choices.

I was also not sure how to process what I'd left behind.

Bill had on jeans and a cotton shirt, not his buckskins, since he was in the middle of loading the hay bales into the barn for winter. It was lunchtime and he was taking a break from haying. The cabin door was inside the woodshed that was built off the side of the cabin, and half-filled with about three cords of wood. A female long-haired cat watched me from the woodpile as her three grey-and-white-tabby-mix, month-old kittens played nearby.

Not more than a few minutes had passed since my arrival when Bill said, "Those kittens will be your winter mittens . . . you can learn how to tan and sew." *Oh, no!* My chest tightened. *I can't do that.* How could I kill cats for mittens? But I knew I couldn't show this weakness, so I kept my mouth shut and nodded.

We went inside where Bill's lunch was on the table, half-eaten. He poured a mug of goat milk for me, telling me it was far better than any milk I had ever tasted (it was in fact warm, sweet, and rich), then offered me bread and some garden greens. The radio above the table on the shelf was on and tuned to some talk show, which felt entirely out of place in a cabin in the middle of this wilderness. The radio personality spewed some blustery political commentary that sounded slanted and mean, and I recoiled from his rant. It felt like a dose of bad medicine.

After lunch, we went out to finish loading the bales in the meadow onto the truck and then stack them into the barn loft. The sweetness of cut field grass permeated the afternoon as Bill pulled an old hay rick behind the truck that dragged the mown grass into rows for bundling. The two guys from the Flathead Valley who worked for the property owners drove behind us and baled the hay. The owners hayed the meadow once or twice a summer. They needed the hay for their cattle down in the valley, but they let Bill put up a couple of tons in the barn for his own animals in trade for his help with the operation. The field doubled as an airstrip, which felt invasive; I had expected total isolation from the world, especially from airplanes and modern power equipment.

We worked through the afternoon, loading fifty-pound

hay bales onto the big farm truck with six-foot side rails and into the barn. I felt tiny against those bales, and had to urge them up with a strength—and maybe some fierce determination—I had not tapped before. I was glad to go right to work, since that meant we didn't have to generate much conversation or wonder how to be with each other. In my new leather gloves, I felt almost ready for my adopted homesteader's life. Now was not the time to show anything but strength.

After we stacked the last bale in the upper level of the barn, Bill said we should clean off in the river. The North Fork of the Flathead River was high with milky, grey-green glacial runoff, fast and cold and as wide as a two-lane highway; more water power than I could manage comfortably, but there was no way I could show my misgivings about swimming across. So, I went up to my new room to change into my mom's nearly antique 1950's swimsuit. I pulled the rear zipper up and adjusted the stays for my chest, and followed Bill's lead.

The river ran down from the northwest next to the cabin, at the most about twenty feet away, and there were places along its bank for washing, drawing water, or fording with horses. When I stepped into the river, the shock and rush of ice water swept my feet out from under me. I started swimming hard to get to the other side. I wanted to be strong enough to go straight across—which might have been possible if I were Johnny Weismuller. Instead, I was carried downstream by the current. It didn't help that my old cotton swimsuit weighed me down. Pulling fast with a freestyle stroke and keeping my eyes on Bill and the shore, I finally got across and stepped onto the rocky landing.

The North Fork of the Flathead River
looking toward Canada

Bill looked at the goose bumps on my arms and laughed. "You look like you've been plucked," he said. We stood in the warmth of the sun a few minutes, then walked a dozen yards back upstream, waded back in, and swam like crazy for home. On the other side, Bill reached out a hand to help me up the bank and then headed toward the big black tank on a platform about six feet above the ground next to the garden that served as a lukewarm shower. The water was steamy compared to the river.

Bill stripped bare and I thought—*Well, I guess I have to do that too.* I felt timid about my body; it looked imperfect to me and I wanted to be attractive to Bill. But I reminded myself that people generally shower without clothes on, and Bill seemed easy and jovial; he had enjoyed a good day, and I felt in those moments that he would watch out for me. I relaxed a little, glad to have landed in Montana, under the shower, after a swim, with Bill.

The shower

After a full day of putting hay up in the barn, a frigid swim across the river, and an open-air shower, I got the tour of the barn, pig pen/chicken coop, garden, and fishing cabins. Every one of Bill's animals was as much a part of the scene as we were. The menagerie included two female goats for milking, Mia and Kimikoi; several chickens and their rooster, Chanticleer; Rastes the mule; Jude, a brown mare; a white-and-tan gelding named Jeremiah, and Bill's special "war pony," Jude's two-year-old stallion colt, named "Ahkee" for the cry of the Peregrine falcon. Bill was very fond of the two white cats, Kriega and Kaya, but he had no affinity for the gray cat and her three young kittens. And there was Woink, a lovely young pig of about thirty pounds who had the run of the place.

I watched Bill milk Mia that first evening before supper, and then gave it a try. "Awkward" is the best word to describe how I wrangled with the teat, but Bill said I would grow the muscle for it. Mia was an older goat, and she was patient and sweet. She had lost her kids and suffered with mastitis the previous winter, and yet she was still giving her milk.

As we walked back to the cabin from the barn, Bill mentioned that Hollis would be coming any time for a few days' visit. I was surprised and excited to hear that. Bill respected Hollis and admired his artwork, and I hoped his visit would ease the tension of this new situation. Hollis knew me through the Carsons, so Bill might accept me more readily.

On the way into the cabin, Bill asked me to grab some kindling, so I loaded up my arms and we went in to start the woodstove to cook dinner. He prepared some kind of stew with onions and bear meat he had canned. He showed me how to make a gravy with goat milk, bear fat, and flour, then told me, "You can cook up supper tomorrow."

It was strange to think that the morning had begun in Kalispell with Sarah, and now, after all the preparation and angst, here I was closing out my first day at Val Halla. It seemed to be going okay so far.

CHAPTER NINE

*T*he only private space I had in the cabin was my bed-room. At the top of the steep, narrow stairs was a room just large enough for a double bed and a cupboard under the window with a shelf for storage, where I put Teddy. Like the rest of the cabin, the room was almost as I had imagined: small and comfortable, but more useful than welcoming. The window faced south onto the meadow, so the sound of the river was muted, but the rooster roused me daily in the pre-dawn morning. There was a bear skin on the bed, and sleeping under the weight of it felt like the strange comfort of the lead apron that protects you from the x-rays at the dentist's office. Even in the summer it was too cool to shed all the fur robes.

Bill's room, just a few feet away on the other side of the stairs, was tiny, like mine. His room always felt like dusk, with one small window above the bed to let in the northern light and the constant song of the river. At times the rushing water was insistent, at other times hushed and calming. It grew quieter after the glacial runoff subsided and the dry heat of July and August set in. On his bed were beaver pelts and a mountain lion hide, along with wool blankets.

During the day I rarely went to my room except to change clothes. But even downstairs, with Bill around, I could escape into my own private space when I sat to write a letter or a journal entry. Before I left, my grandmother, Didi, had given me a blank book with an Italian floral print in blue and white on the cover. I had never kept a journal, but I knew this experience would be something I wouldn't want to fade with time, and the journal would be a place where I could work out my thoughts. My intention was to write in the journal daily, but the entries were sporadic, reflecting my reactions to Bill and my place in his world. I wrote the first entry the day after I arrived.

July 1, 1974, Monday

This valley is the most beautiful yet that I have seen—time has etched a wild sawtooth range of mountains running north south, and hills surround and fortify a valley holding the waters now somewhat muddy still, of the North Fork of the Flathead. Cabin is so close that at night the river whispers and gushes by Bill's bedroom window. After haying, and being introduced to all the animals in the neighborhood, bear meat was cooked for sup while we swatted and slapped at those nasty mosquitoes finding a juicy place for their own sup. Would have liked much to leap into the river this morning—too cold tho—but yesterday proved an invigorating little swim for sure—five strokes takes a body near 50 feet down river.

Now the room is swaying with a tune Bill's playing—he plays like a dream—sounds almost like Debussy, but not so gentle. I recognize it—so beautiful—sky's clouded up and the day was cool —tho I did try to brave a swim at the beaver ponds—there I had a hunch Bill and Ahkee might ride up on me, and sure enough a few minutes after I heard Ahkee's cry they came fast to the end of the runway, riding like the wind. So badly I wanted to climb on and charge across the field with them, but now I haven't the strength— and Rastes had no halter or bridle. Maybe Hollis, Bill and I will go off on a ride together.

Yesterday when I walked up to the cabin, and knew Bill was inside as I could hear him, felt sure he was giving me a test—see maybe if I had the guts to walk right in.

Still Hollis hasn't appeared—but we made bread and with a little luck it came out ok.

BREAD

put 1 & 1/3 tblspns yeast & some sugar into warm water—let sit covered in warm place. Then scald 3 & 1/2 cups milk in pan —adding 6 tblspns sugar, 2 tblspns salt, 4 tblspns shortening or grease.

Have flour warmed in oven (white, soy, wheat)—then mix in big bowl the scalded milk adding flour until a pancake consistency is reached—add yeast (eggs 2-3 can be added just before this)—add rest of flour—knead & let rise till doubles in size—slice into loaves—grease pans & bread, rolls or whatever —let rise in pan till doubles in size—then bake at about 350-400 until golden brown, keeping fire embers hot but not burning or blazing. Cool on rack, use grease on top to keep crust soft—cover with rag until cool, then put in plastic.

other good mixtures
- *rice—cheese & egg*
- *corn fritters (or berry)*
- *corned moose hash*
- *soy bean soup (with pork)*

Seminole Fry Bread
1 cup flour (white & whole wheat)

1 1/2 *teaspoon salt*

2 *teaspoon baking powder*

2 *tablespoon sugar*

1/2 *cup milk*

put into hot grease after made into small squares.

Those first few days, Bill spent time showing me the routine of the daily chores. I would be responsible for lighting the fire in the woodstove every morning, tending the animals, most of the cooking and washing, and helping with the garden. "You can't risk losing a finger," he warned, "or waste food." It felt more like an admonition than a lesson. Every aspect of life encompassed a realm of activities. Every chore had a peak efficiency level, every resource had a limit (no more than four squares of toilet paper per trip to the outhouse), and use beyond that limit meant waste.

Some of the chores were easy, while others were more of a trial. When you hold a piece of kindling halfway down as it rests on the stump and swing a sharp hatchet through the end to split it into a sliver for the stove, there is a rhythm and strange sort of satisfaction. I felt competent and a little victorious when I could wash a whole pan of dishes with one kettle of hot water. There was no running water and no drain, so there was a prescribed method, and it was the kind of challenge I could manage.

I also loved the magic of turning flour, salt, milk, and oil into a wonderful loaf of bread. Meat was more of a mystery. There were quart jars of canned meat, including bear, elk, mountain lion, and corned moose on the shelf, and I had no idea what to create with that meat. I ended up making stews, usually, with garden vegetables and roots. It did not meet the standard of Mom's cooking, but we ate well. Bill reminded me more than once that I was using his food store. He was clear that he would not put up with a free-loader, and that the chores I was doing were a way to earn my keep. I never knew how to answer, so I just doubled down on my efforts to please him.

The physical work outside—pulling weeds around young garden plants, feeding the animals, or refitting the stone path that Woink upturned with his snout—felt productive and peaceful. Eventually I would become comfortable milking the goats, and I'd develop some forearm muscle to show for it.

But not everything was as simple. I would come to dread doing the laundry with the old gas-powered washing machine in the yard. It was touchy, and noisy, and the wringer was semi-functional, so all of the jeans, shirts, and sheets had to be wrung by hand, and it was hard to wrestle with them by myself. Lugging the five-gallon container of river water up the bank and into the cabin was just about the limit of what I could muscle, and invariably I sloshed out more than a few drops.

Cleaning was more meditative and rewarding. As a young girl I was always organizing my books and toys and papers, and liked things to be just so. I made my bed with hospital corners, like Mom showed me. And I had always helped in the kitchen or the yard, happiest when I was busy with a task or project. Mom was intensely organized and tidy, and my siblings and I had absorbed those tendencies.

The day I arrived to start my new life in Montana, I immediately noticed the disarray and dust and felt compelled to clean the cabin. The next morning, after I finished with my chores, while Bill was busy outside, I spent a couple of hours dusting and straightening shelves—putting like with like, washing surfaces. The wall closest to the yard had a window where Bill kept his work desk with the typewriter and his beadwork projects. I stacked the papers, cleaned off the desk surface, and made a neat pile of the tools. Under the other window on that wall was a big pine-topped counter and kitchen workspace on top of a storage cupboard; I arranged the pots and pans in the cupboard and cleared the clutter on the work surface. Between those windows was a long cupboard with the plates and glasses, and above that a set of shelves that held the books and all of the canned meats and vegetables. I organized and straightened the books and dusted every jar. It was enormously satisfying to make sense of the chaos, and I was glad to do something to help Bill.

After he finished his outside chores, Bill came in and exclaimed, "Well, haven't you been busy!" But he seemed displeased. I was, after all, essentially re-ordering his world. The non-verbal don't-touch-my-things message was not friendly. I was careful after that to just maintain a tidy, clean space, and to leave his things alone.

That episode left me feeling nervous about my role with Bill and what I could do to be useful; I realized that it was best for him to take the lead. Later that afternoon, he asked me to help him with a task: he had to sharpen a new knife on the grinding stone and needed me to turn the crank on the grinding wheel. I was thrilled—this put me in the category of Partner. I was glad to be able to help him.

Bill told me where to stand, how to place my feet, and to use my whole body in a rocking motion so I wouldn't tire my arms. He probably could have turned the crank himself if he hadn't torn open his hand a few days earlier, before I arrived, while shoeing Jude. A nail had caught the meat of his palm when the horse jerked her hoof. He'd sewn his hand with eight neat stiches, and told me that stitching a hand was a snap compared to piecing together some of the soldiers he'd tried to doctor in Vietnam. I shuddered a little thinking about being sewn together and whether I could do it myself, but supposed adrenaline might chase the fear, and reason would expose the alternative: a bad, festering wound.

CHAPTER TEN

*W*hen Hollis drove his truck onto the property July 3, Bill met him outside with a hearty handshake. Hollis was a calm, kind man with a bit of a southern drawl, and I breathed easier when he arrived. The two men joked and showed off their powder guns and I could tell it was good for Bill to have an ally and male compadre.

Hollis had brought a sketchbook to do some charcoal pencil studies of Bill in his furs and buckskins, and his drawings were elegant and beautiful. Hollis was an artist who could see and translate that seeing without effort—he used charcoal to shade, highlight, or express fur, skin, and metal so simply.

I stayed in the background and listened as they talked and Bill shared details about how to brain-tan a hide or prepare blanks of steel to shape them into knives. Hollis was fascinated with the brain-tanning process, and just about everything else Bill had accomplished to survive in the wilderness. His drawings and sculptures often portrayed the mountain men of old in their trappings, and this was a chance for him to see and touch that world.

One of the things Hollis wanted to learn was how to throw a tomahawk. He had brought one with him so he and Bill could practice together. Bill had a huge wheel of a log set up as the target, and I joined them one morning to learn how to throw. A tomahawk is lighter than a hatchet, with a

straight handle and an almost triangular head. Bill's tomahawk was a fine piece of work so I practiced with Hollis's,
just in case. To throw, you stand at the appropriate distance for the tomahawk to turn in the air one or more times
and land with a satisfying *thunk!* in the stump. By the time
we took a break, I had learned to throw the tomahawk
cleanly at one turn and had almost succeeded at two turns;
Bill and Hollis even gave me kudos for a job well done.

The next day, when the two of them went up the river
to shoot at targets with their powder guns, they invited me
along. I loved target shooting but only had experience with
Pappy's .22, and with a bow and arrow at camp, so I went
along to try out a powder pistol. We were aiming for rocks
along the bank about fifty yards away. Hollis guided me to
a sitting position with my arms anchored so I could steady
the gun. When I pulled the trigger, the impact kicked me
backward with surprising force. I didn't hit my target, but
thought that with practice I might. Guns were familiar to
me since Mom and Dad had always had shotguns. They
shot at clay pigeons for practice and occasionally shot
game, mostly grouse or pheasant.

That evening, Bill and Hollis laughed and chatted as I
cooked, and at dinner they included me in the conversation,
mostly thanks to Hollis. I felt comfortable and happy that I
had something to add to the evening banter; I felt like an
equal. Maybe Bill would see me as more of a partner after
this visit, but it was hard to tell. Hollis would leave in a day
or two, and I'd need to find a way to retain some of the energy and lightheartedness we all felt that night.

Mail came up from the postal station in Polebridge twice a week, on Tuesdays and Fridays. The mailbox was out on the road near the border post, across the meadow and up past the spring where we could draw fresh water. I intended to keep my promise to write home often, so I sent a letter to my parents just a few days after I arrived, on the Fourth of July, while Hollis was visiting. Even though I shared thoughts with them that I could not address with Bill, I wanted to sound confidant and content. I had pushed away from their world but was still tethered to it; I wanted to hear about the day-to-day at home. And I missed them.

Dear Mom and Dad,

Right now we are sitting on the bank overlooking the river and waiting for the canoe racers to go by—the river is mighty cold, but if it gets hot enough today maybe we'll swim it; first day I got here we swam down a ways before hopping under the shower, and it's about time to clean off right today, 'cause I'm grungy.

Well, so far, I've needed every ounce of strength, especially in milking old Mia—she's very patient with me though—but Kimikoi, the other nanny, is feisty with me, she'll rear up and pretend to be fierce, but she doesn't have horns so I'm safe. Every morning we're up around 7, then the hog and chickens are to be fed. (The hog's name is Woink—he'll be slaughtered in a few months.) Woink is the biggest pig, he snarfs around at your feet when the milk pail is in hand, and he doesn't even mind if you push him away or anything. Ahkee is Bill's stallion, and he's so gentle and smooth and neck reins beautifully.

(Canoes just went by, all two-man boats; the river is high and fast so the 80-90 miles should be easy for most of them).

So far, the most important thing is not to waste anything, and to utilize time well and spare yourself spent energy in doing chores —and to keep a fire going the right way still has to be learned, but I've picked up so much in my few days here that it's hard for me to remember it all.

This is a fantastically beautiful valley, a high jagged chain of mountains runs north-south on the far side of the river, and we are in the first valley west of the continental divide—first day here I helped Bill finish clearing the new mown hay off the runway and put it in the barn, then, that night (since I was a guest) we had bear meat and m-m is it good! Also I've learned how to make Seminole fry cakes, pancakes and most importantly, bread. Am becoming stronger and more proficient at chopping wood, too.

Bill's working on a new knife and so I've been cranking the wheel that grinds it down, and sometimes when I thought I couldn't grind any more I'd have to keep going because that is a small part of endurance. Mostly Bill has been doing the talking when he's teaching, and then he tells stories and about his time in Vietnam and at home—

Hollis just got here—looking good, but boy did Bill jump on him when he saw he still had cigarettes in his pocket. You see, Bill, when he decides he doesn't like something—that's it. He's so self-confident and proud that if I try to defend myself on a subject, forget it—and when I make a mistake, like using rancid grease to make my bread yesterday ooeee—it's to the pig stall for me. No, it's not that bad at all, he's been explaining everything he knows about animals, gardens, everything, and he never lets me forget how long it took him to learn, and how many mistakes he made before he saw how to do things the easiest, best, way.

The walls are hung with lion skins, elk, hawk feathers, antlers hold back the curtains and support the guns, one of which is a beautiful inlaid Hawken rifle. Beaded quiver and antlers carved into scent bottles, powder horns, and knife cases. Incredible.

Weeded today in the garden, where the strawberry plants are growing—and to see the berries on the way it's a pleasure to care for the plants—Slowly I'm learning to cook, but I've blown it a few times, that's for sure, but I've managed to turn out every meal ok, with a little grief from my friends if it goes funny.

Last night I slept under a beaver pelt and a mountain lion, because Hollis slept in my bed with two grizzly hides—talk about warm. Maybe today I'll get to shoot Hollis' pistol, it's a powder gun —and last night the two of them were shooting their powder rifles across the river—too loud for my liking. The people who own this land were up here for the Fourth of July weekend, shooting firecrackers, kids screaming around, craziness, it really distorted the whole atmosphere—but they'll be gone in another day or so, and everything will be quiet again.

From upstairs Bill just brought down a whole collection of furs, some made into hats, some into vests, and some whole—like wolves, lynx, cross-fox, mink & cat. Bill's all dressed in his fur hat, (one of 'em) & his mitts and they're joking around, I guess men get silly too sometimes.

Tell everyone hello for me, because there is not time yet to write, I'm spending my time watching, learning. I love you both very much.

Annie xoxoxo

After Hollis left, Bill's jovial mood dropped away, and I felt a little empty too. All that was exciting about beginnings was fading; I was alone with Bill again, and thinking about how to step more completely into this new life. There was plenty to do and learn about how to manage chores, so I simply settled into that routine as my first order of business.

But the physical work was only part of the process of joining Bill's world. I also needed to find an emotional strength and commitment that seemed elusive still. The simple tasks boosted my confidence but Bill was urging me to do some things independent of him, including learning how to do beadwork, ride, and to read more. He could see that I was filling my days with busywork, and that aggravated him on some level. In his letters he had let me know that he was not willing to hold my hand or be held back by my fears or inability to manage the lifestyle, and I now felt pressure to do the things he was suggesting without really knowing how to take them on. The mixed message about taking care of chores and establishing an independent and creative realm for myself was confusing. How could I possibly manage to sit for long enough to draw, or play the piano without feeling that I was neglecting the garden or cooking chores? I was intimidated about Bill watching me attempt those skills, and afraid of failing before I even tried. Even so, I gave myself a pep talk and pictured riding alone, or creating something, and nudged myself toward that goal.

✗

CHAPTER ELEVEN

I knew I would get a letter soon from Mom and Dad and, in fact, our first letters crossed in the mail. On Tuesday, July 9, as I waited for the mail like a kid at camp, I whittled a face and my name into a stick with my pen knife while I sat on a rock near the road, planning to put it in a box of keepsakes of my Montana life.

The mail truck came up the road, and when I met the driver, he handed me a letter from Mom.

Saturday, July 6th

Dearest Annie,

I think of you constantly—wondering. It's hard for me to imagine how your new way of life is affecting you physically and emotionally and how it will affect your future. Do try to describe it to me when you have a chance. I'm sitting on the terrace and the birds are making such a racket in the cherry trees that I can hardly concentrate; magpies, robins, flickers & some other variety. I've picked most of the cherries, however. Annie Collins had a seven-pound girl on Jen's birthday! All's well.

At the end of Geof's letter he has a message for you. "I want to just say one word to Annie perchance I don't have an opportunity before she embarks on her adventure. Annie, I admire your courage and hope for the best for you. What you are doing is beyond most people's strength and if it is not successful do not consider yourself defeated; you are shooting at an awfully high goal. Dress warmly and best of luck. If you're near a post office let me know how it goes."

Moonie took most everything left over from your garage sale except for the trunk, etc.

Take care my sweet; I love and miss you.Mom
p.s. Do you need anything?

Hollis had left a few days earlier to go back to Denver and Bill had headed down to Kalispell in his truck to get some supplies for a pack trip he was planning to take in the next few weeks through Glacier Park to Browning, Montana. Bill had carved the image of a bobcat into the butt of an elk antler for a man who owned the cat and he planned to deliver it to his friend by horseback.

When he left for supplies, Bill said he intended to drive down and back in a day, but he didn't come home that night, so I was alone for the first time. The next day, after I finished the chores, I wrote a long letter to my parents. The sky was volatile, with dark rain clouds massing and pouring toward the glacial peaks to the east. As I sat looking out the window from Bill's desk, the sun came from behind a cloud, lighting up grasses and leaves to glow against a dark sky. "Oh how I love green & grey," I wrote.

Sitting on top of the desk was a completed beadwork project that Bill had been working on for some time. It was an otter tail that Bill had sewn into a sheath for his new knife and then beaded with a black, white, and red diamond pattern that was striking. I described it for my parents as "spectacular . . . intricate although simple at the same time," and mentioned that I planned to try my hand at beadwork.

I filled them in on what was growing in the garden, the weather, and the horses, who were constantly talked to and loved by Bill. To that I added, "He really knows their wavelengths too, it's like the sixth sense or something." I included random notes about baking successes, my increased speed milking the goats, and of course a note about Woink:

> *I should be building myself through exercise & running because it would be mighty helpful for when Woink gets bigger. You should see the struggle keeping him away from his grain while I'm trying to pour the milk in—and he's not yet half the weight he will be! We have a running joke about Woink, anything I cook, if it looks like a mess, Bill asks why I cook for Woink instead of him. Well anyway.*

I wrote about the few days Hollis had spent with us, thinking it might be some solace for my parents that Bill had friends and we were not so isolated as they might have imagined. I also thought Mom and Dad would appreciate that Bill and Hollis enjoyed a shared interest in old guns.

After I explained Bill's upcoming trip and errand for supplies, I wondered on paper why he'd not yet made it back from Kalispell. Once he left for his pack trip, I told my parents, I would be taking care of the animals and property on my own, for a week or maybe more, to protect it from "the people in the valley (who) make up lies about the 'Dirty hippie,' Bill—and now they're talking about me I'm sure." Bill had sown the seeds of distrust, and I'd decided to believe him. His attitude went against my feelings about people, which was that most folks were decent and just living their own lives. It occurred to me that maybe Bill was protecting his privacy, or his image, by determining that everyone outside of his chosen circle was the enemy. But maybe he was right. Since I had made a point of joining him, it was easier to adopt his position than try to take a different stance.

I segued into a discourse about Bill, further cementing his diatribe as truth in my own mind. His dystopian spin on the culture I came from was a strange path to follow, but I tried to try to justify it with my parents:

> *Often times he can tell what I'm thinking and will tell me exactly what's on my mind. The stories he has to tell! All about Vietnam & high school and how he disliked and mistrusts others . . . how arrogant he is! BUT he is the man he wants to be and judges others on how they judge themselves . . . He's very sensitive and conscientious and can see right through men & their foul ways—in a way it may seem as though I'm being brainwashed to think the way he does, but really, he is so right in everything he says and does that I can't dispute his mind. There's so much to grasp of what he says that I can barely lay claim to just one idea long enough to question it.*

Finally, I addressed the message from my brother, who had suggested that it would not be a defeat if I decided to return home. I pushed back, arguing that returning would mean rejoining the "lying, stupid 'combine' system under a failing government" that I was hell-bent to leave. Bill had accused me of coming to Val Halla to just sample his lifestyle, like a dilettante, and I did not want to consider myself that way, as someone doing this "just to see if I can do it." I told my parents, "I love it and want to be here, so unless I fail Bill there is no reason to leave."

I needed to tell them that I appreciated all they had done for me, but offered a look back at what I had left to justify where I'd landed. The list of what was wrong with my old life included a not-so-subtle admission about drinking parties with friends that I had been part of—"not that I'm innocent, but now I'm out of it." It was a way to let them know that I was stepping away from my own trouble. And I tore into the institution of marriage, especially in the "white culture," calling it a farce or a way to secure funding in retirement. The rant came from my own discomfort with relationships, and those I had watched in my parents' generation. This was naïve, since I didn't have the experience to make these claims. Nevertheless, I stated that the "Indians complemented each other, worked with and for each other," and that there was "definitely something wrong with the white race." In living with Bill, I reasoned, I was avoiding being part of that culture. At least for the time being.

This insistent and negative letter to Mom and Dad was a reaction to the notion that I might not be able to handle my new situation with Bill. That possibility felt like a huge step backward, and I was afraid of that result, especially since I had put my parents and others through so much in my plan to take on this lifestyle. I had rejected options like going to college, working elsewhere for a year, or joining the Peace Corps. Although I didn't consciously process it, there was an underlying sense that I had already failed in my life at home, and I had to make this plan work.

Besides, I had only just arrived.

CHAPTER TWELVE

*F*ood procurement, preparation, and storage was a constant effort and consideration. Bill supplied himself with fifty-pound bags of onions, dried beans, grain, salt, sugar, and some other staples a couple of times a year when he ventured into Kalispell. He planted a slew of vegetables, raised animals, and hunted. The garden was roughly twenty by thirty feet and was densely planted with salad greens, root crops, strawberries, peas, and onions.

Looking west toward the barn from the garden

All of the food from the garden would be preserved by canning or storing it in bins of sand in the root house. The only garden produce you couldn't keep were the salad greens, and when we harvested the first tender lettuce leaves, they tasted heavenly. The root vegetables, including carrots, parsnips, onion, rutabaga, and turnips, would keep in the cool sand and constant 40 degrees of the root house through the winter, so Bill always planted an abundance of root crops.

That summer I tasted rutabaga (Bill called them "rooty beggars"), parsnip, and turnip for the first time, since they'd never been part of our family dinner fare. The earthy sweet denseness of rutabaga did not turn soft as I had expected, like a sweet potato in a stew, and the slightly bitter flavor of a turnip surprised me.

It took some finessing to master the temperature control on the wood stove, and Bill would express frustration when I burned something, or if it took forever to cook. He said women tended to load the woodbox much too often. *Hmmmm.* Even after he explained what size of wood splits to use and how to regulate burn intensity with air flow, it took me some time to finally get a sense of balance with the stove.

Bill had a couple of antique pioneer cookbooks he referred to for canning and preserving instructions, and I used them occasionally, but I mostly enjoyed trying to be a little creative. Food was an important part of my sharing with Bill, and I was discovering that I truly liked to cook. Both of us were interested in the science and process of cooking, and I was eager to learn more about a whole foods diet. One of the cookbooks on his shelf was dated 1908, and Bill enjoyed reading bits out loud about different foods and cooking methods and how they affect our health. I was already aware that too much sugar, fat, or refined food was hard on the liver and unhealthy in general, but was interested to learn about how milk sugars affected digestion. Of course, that cookbook was almost seventy years behind in research, but some of the science behind it was still relevant.

There was a right way to do everything. Bill taught me how to be more efficient with a large knife, what order to add ingredients in a dish, and most importantly how to make the most of available foods. He was adamant about efficiency and avoiding waste. I scraped out eggshells, and every grain of flour ended up in the bread when I finally learned the process. Bill stressed how well "the last woman" had learned to use every resource so completely. He was proud that he'd taught her to be efficient and that she had accomplished so much on her own. He bragged on her behalf that she could easily heft a fifty-pound bag of grain—double the amount I had just struggled with. I hoped to become that strong too.

Most of our dinners included meat, a starch, and a vegetable. I often sautéed the meat or added a gravy, and I cooked with a healthy amount of bear grease. The grease was Crisco-like; white and semi-solid since it had been rendered, or cooked. We ate well; I would gain more than ten pounds over the summer, which was a negative for Bill and for me—it meant that I was not in control, and I was eating up his resources. Our meals and the focus on food preparation was so much different than I had experienced at home or at school, and with less physical activity than I needed, eventually my overalls and jeans grew snug and I started wearing Bill's old jeans. He was kind to not say anything but I knew he was watching.

Bread-baking was surprisingly rewarding. I did ruin at least one batch of bread, but soon my loaves were light and flavorful. Bill even told me that my bread was better than his! I loved the process: Bring milk to a near boil, add the grease, salt, and sugar, and cool to finger warm. Add yeast and once it bubbles some, start to mix in the flour until it becomes a blob of dough. Turn it onto the board and knead as you add the flour, folding the dough with a rocking motion that becomes almost meditative. Bill taught me that once the dough did not stick to your hand if you held it and turned your hand upside down, it was elastic and ready to rise.

Fresh-out-of-the-oven bread is right up there with good chocolate. Bill had put up jars of huckleberry jam, and for a treat we would spread it sparingly on warm bread, savoring every bite.

We did not have refrigeration; we kept food in a cabinet built into the north side of the cabin that stayed relatively cool and was alright for storing vegetables, baked goods, or milk for short periods. It wasn't a good place for any other animal-based foods, so we usually cooked a meal and ate all of it to avoid food storage problems, but sometimes there was the inevitable leftover bit of something. Not long after I arrived, when we had visitors from the fishing cabins who stayed for a meal, I prepared deviled eggs, since we had an egg surplus. There was plenty of other food and we didn't finish the eggs, so they went into the "cold box." It wasn't cold enough. Within a day or so, I thought about the deviled eggs for a meal addition, but when I opened the cold box door and looked at them closely, I saw that they were wriggling with maggots—ugh! More food I had to toss.

Cooking a meal was more or less forgiving, but canning on a wood stove is challenging and rigorous. I had not tried my hand at it yet; I assumed that at some point I would. When Bill had a surplus of fresh meat that he could not eat, he often canned it. You can only keep fresh meat for so long unless it's the dead of winter and you have a safe place to hang it, frozen and away from other hungry critters. There were two or three dozen jars of canned moose, bear, elk, and even mountain lion lined up on top of the cupboard. They looked like preserved specimens in a laboratory, and the first few times I cooked with the canned meats I had to remind myself that there was no formaldehyde or fetal pig in those jars.

Over time, I grew comfortable with most of the chores. I learned a few cooking basics, so Bill didn't need to coach my every move. Our daily routine included getting up at daybreak to get the fire started in the cookstove. The next chore for me was milking. Mia was my pal because she was so sweet and responsive. She and Kimi would follow me to the barn, where Mia would jump onto her wooden milking bench to eat her oats. Kimi was not producing milk then, so I'd put her in another stall with her feed so she couldn't bother us. It was amazing to watch and feel the muscles for particular tasks develop. To milk, you pinch the teat hard in the crook between your thumb and forefinger, then squeeze your fingers into your palm while you push up against the bag, and the muscles in the forearm feel the work. I hoped that I didn't hurt her.

Old Mia gave about a quart of milk a day. On the way back to the cabin, Kimi would butt at me, and once or twice she made me spill almost a whole pail. We always had a surplus of milk, though, so I was less fearful of spilling a little. What we didn't use I gave to Woink. The goat's milk tasted sweet and a little tangy, like yogurt. It wasn't as rich as cow's milk, and more easily digested. I loved drinking that milk; it tasted of the meadow and the mountains.

Mia in front of the cabin

After milking, I fed the chickens and Woink. For Woink's breakfast I cooked barley or oats with milk or leftover vegetables. He'd wait at the kitchen door and follow me to his pen, nudging me along. Woink shared the fenced yard with the chickens; he had one corner where we'd made a mud puddle for him, and the far corner was his outhouse. Pigs are sensitive and particular, and I thought Woink was especially intelligent. He was just a little guy when I arrived, about knee-high, but within a month he had doubled in size. He had the run of the place and was welcome everywhere but in the cabin, although he did visit occasionally. Sometimes he would play with Rastes the mule, racing around his legs and trying to get Rastes to play chase with him. Occasionally Rastes would get into the game, and it was amazing to watch that big mule wheel around in a mock threat while Woink dodged and ran to his other side, then dashed into his pen and splashed down in his mud puddle. He was curious and affectionate, and I thought he had a smile on his face sometimes. We would scratch him behind his ears, and when he was big enough, I could even ride him a few paces—not that *he* thought of that as a good time.

Of course, I knew we were raising Woink for meat, but I did not let that thought linger too long. I loved and enjoyed him, like you would a good dog. Bill cared for him, too, and called him Brother Woink because he claimed that Woink had more integrity and wisdom than most preachers.

Once the animals were fed, I cooked breakfast—usually eggs with bread or oatmeal—and we drank chamomile tea from dried flowers Bill harvested around the yard during the summer. After the breakfast dishes were done, the day would unfold. Some days were taken up with fixing tools, weeding the garden, scraping hides, making bread, or doing laundry. On others we might venture out to ride, hunt, pick huckleberries, or cut wood.

One afternoon not long after Hollis left, Bill told me to put the animals in their pens so we could leave for a couple of hours to go grouse hunting. It was not grouse season and Bill didn't have a license, but he'd decided it would be a treat to have fresh meat. We were eating mostly canned elk and moose, since it was summer—too warm to keep fresh meat around. I was simply glad for an adventure.

We drove a few miles south and west on an old fire road. Bill brought only a rope and some slingshots he had made with hickory branches and surgical tubing with a square of leather elk hide to pull back with the stone. He'd given me one that was easier to pull back than the one he used, and I had practiced shooting with it but was certainly no deadeye.

Grouse don't move much; they sit on a branch and remain quite still—thinking, I suppose, that they can't be seen, but it makes them a steady target. Bill instructed me to gather round pebbles the size of grapes to hand to him, and he would shoot. He hit three or four grouse within a half hour that afternoon. It amazed me how he could spot them up in the trees, then kill them with a slingshot.

We stowed the grouse in the well of the spare tire in the bed of the truck and threw a tarp over them. I thought it odd that he was being so careful to conceal them since we were so far from anywhere—but just as we started back out on the fire road, the border guard and our neighbor, Bob, drove up. We rarely saw him or his wife, Irene, but there he was. Bob was friendly and got out of his truck to say hello and chat a bit. I raised my eyebrows and wondered how Bill knew we would meet someone—an official, no less. As we pulled away, he turned to me with a big grin, pleased with himself for outsmarting the enemy.

When we got back to the cabin, we plucked and cleaned

the grouse, then Bill cut them apart. We rolled the tiny breasts—each one about the size of an egg yolk—in flour seasoned with salt and some herbs, and quickly seared them. The meat was sweet and tender.

As we enjoyed the fresh, wild game, a memory about a meal of grouse with Mom and Dad came to me. I was six or seven and it was a clear fall day. My parents went grouse hunting up at our cabin, and they took me with them to the woods' edge above the beaver ponds where they had seen grouse the previous day. They shot a few birds and I helped them gut and clean them near the beaver ponds. We had to be careful eating them that night since there was the odd bit of buckshot left in the breast. The meat was dark, delicate, and rich.

That distant memory seemed like a link to my present life, as if it had prepared me in some way for all of these new experiences with Bill.

CHAPTER THIRTEEN

$\mathcal{J}$uly 10 was hot. It was early afternoon, and I was weeding the persistent invasive grass that encroached on the garden. When I looked up, I saw Bill come from the barn with two huge inner tubes and a big grin. "Annie gal, go put on your swim outfit and we'll take a ride."

Oh boy! Bill wanted to play, and he'd addressed me as a friend. I pulled on Mom's swimsuit, reaching to zip the last two inches up the back, and wore my sneakers because the river was so rocky and slippery.

We stepped into the water below the cabin where there was a slope in for crossing and hopped into our tubes. The chill was welcome. Bill bounced along in front of me, spinning in his tube and pushing off the few rocks that were newly exposed. We had been floating along for about ten minutes when I heard Bill yell, and it was not good. He had reached out to pull himself around a low branch hanging over the river and had pulled his shoulder out of the socket.

My internal reaction was one of panic, but I tried to keep calm outwardly. This was serious; the disjointed shoulder looked awful, and he was in so much pain it frightened me. We got out of the river and managed to get up the bank. I carried both inner tubes as we walked back through the meadow toward the cabin. He went directly over to his chin-up bar and had me pull a stump over for him to stand on so he could push his arm up and grab the bar, then he dropped to a hang. From several feet away I heard the *pop!* when the shoulder snapped back into place, and Bill's yelp as he fell to the ground. Afterward I helped him immobilize the arm and shoulder in a sling we made from a torn shirt.

The incident put us both on edge. He was trying to prepare for his pack trip through Glacier Park to Browning, and I was not yet confident enough to take everything on by myself, since I had not even been there for two weeks. His frustration with me was exaggerated by his injury, and I wondered if I would be able to override my feelings of inadequacy and doubt to prove that I could manage. Those thoughts kept cycling in ruts in my head and I was not sure how to break free of them. I wished for a way to soothe him and felt that if he would guide me, I could help. When he did ask me to do things for him, it eased the frustration some. *Nothing is forever*, I would remind myself.

A few days after Bill's accident, I noticed a car across the meadow at the little cabin next to a small creek below the embankment. Bill took off to go visit the folks there, and came back to tell me that we had been invited to join them for a fried chicken supper.

Later in the afternoon, we walked over and I met Joe and Flo Nelson. I immediately felt comfortable with them. The wood-burned sign over the door of their one-room twelve-by-sixteen-foot cabin read MOOSE CITY. They must have been a little over sixty years old, and Bill mentioned as we walked over that they came up to their cabin on occasional weekends in the summer since Joe had not yet retired from the small hydropower plant in Bigfork, two hours south near Kalispell, where he was the manager.

Before I even said hello, Flo, in a brash sort of way, said, "Oh, you're a brave girl to come live with Bill!"—with

Bill standing right there. I guessed she could get away with that. Clearly, they had a relationship that included respect, and some deference, and I gleaned that she saw right through his posturing and self-righteous veneer. She also reminded him that here she was, feeding him again, and he had *never* invited them for dinner at his cabin.

Flo was tough and honest and didn't mince words. She had a wry sense of humor and stories to tell about anything and everything: what animals they saw on the drive, how hot it had been in the valley and what that did for the farmers, the improvements Joe had made in the volunteer fire department where he was the fire chief, and what the other property owners were up to. She liked to talk and never ran out of words.

Joe was kind, a gentleman, and evenhanded. He was quiet, and very present, and seemed entirely nonjudgmental. He had a way of smiling and showing what was in his heart with his eyes. Both he and Flo had voices that sounded soft and round, but with a sandy texture. Joe spoke with a musical but halting rhythm, maybe more like quiet chanting. When Flo talked her voice ran up and down the scale but often settled in the middle and drove the sentence. Flo had some Northwest Native American blood, and I could sometimes detect that vocal lilt I'd heard when Native Americans spoke.

I felt at home with them right away, as if I had known them forever, and was relieved that they were part of our lives in a peripheral way. Maybe I sensed they'd keep an eye on me.

Supper with Joe & Flo at their Moose City cabin
Photo credit: Catherine Atkinson

CHAPTER FOURTEEN

9 assumed that sex would be part of the arrangement
with Bill. We did not sleep together when I first arrived,
and I appreciated that he didn't approach me immediately,
but I was certain that at some point he would. He hadn't
hinted at any attraction, but I hoped that at least I wasn't
unattractive to him. With a short haircut and wire-rim
glasses, and usually dressed in overalls, I looked more like
someone's kid sister than a good-looking woman. I didn't
doubt that he'd been hoping for someone more feminine.

The third night after my arrival, as I was getting to
sleep, I felt Bill crawl into bed next to me. He asked if that
was all right, and whether I was using any birth control.
Yes, I told him quietly, and yes. There was not much else I
could say; we barely knew each other. Physically, I felt as if
I had been ready to make love for a long time. Intercourse
was not a mystery to me; even though I was technically a
virgin, I was not unfamiliar with my body and the pleasure
of touch, and I had enjoyed the kiss and play that I had already explored. I wanted my first "real" sexual experience to
be loving and magical, and rich with passion. Bill did not
spend much time with touch, however; he did not kiss me,
was direct, and didn't linger much. I only felt a little pain,
but not the excitement or the loss of ego that was supposed
to happen with the sacred act of lovemaking. He was gentle
enough, but not tender. Why should he be? I was a self-in-
vited guest.

The difference in our age and the vast expanse between us in our life experiences was a real barrier; I would have to earn his respect, his friendship, and his love. And it seemed that every aspect of my presence came with some negative, however small, so it would take time and a great effort on my part to become a positive in his world. I did not feel like there was a way or a reason to talk to him about my brother-in-law.

Neither of us spoke until afterward, when he asked me if that had been my first experience. He seemed thoughtful, or maybe considerate, as we lay there for a few minutes quietly. And then he left to sleep in his own bed.

My letters to Mom and Dad revealed some of the doubts and discomfort that I was feeling in this first couple of weeks with Bill, but I couldn't share the details of my sex life with them. Sex was not exactly a taboo subject with Mom; after all, she saw me through my first exam for a prescription for the Pill. But neither of us was sure how to have a conversation about the act itself, or the fact that I was engaged in it. My journal, therefore, would have to be my sounding board as I tried to sort out this complicated emotional realm I had entered; it was the only place where I could unfold those deeper thoughts and describe my inner landscape.

July 12, 1974

So far, I've been here almost two weeks and written but few words —nor have I done any drawing, because the learning & chores take so long to do and the meals last forever. Oh god the food! I've never felt so overstuffed as I do here, because there's always so much of everything (but definitely not a surplus of huckleberry jam) and nothing is to be wasted.

Yes, already the sex has come into it, I never expected it so soon. But I don't like it very well at all, probably because I'm scared and not in love with the man—that could be why, but I'm not sure. Sometimes I feel as an imposition to him, and he gets impatient when I don't do something right—because he's always right. Today listening to a program about a jazz & blues pianist named Fats— he said he didn't like the music because there was nothing to it. And that there are wars going on, but if he's chosen to put himself apart from the world affairs, why does he act so? He knocks Archie Bunker as if he doesn't have some in him, and I'm afraid to challenge his position because he'd say "Didn't I ask you not to question what I do and why?" but then he says—"I got here by questioning." He confuses me.

And now he's hurt his shoulder and is restless and wants to go, and that's not putting him in the best of moods—maybe he'll be able to leave next week.

This place is beautiful, and this lifestyle couldn't be more peaceful and real, but already I find myself longing for family and more of a child's life, at least for a couple of years.

True, I never feel better than when running on a horse, but this is Bill's life, he's built everything in it, and has his own special way of doing things that makes me feel suppressed somehow. I remember the family and friend times up at the cabin, and long for those, maybe I'm afraid because I don't really know where I'm headed, and wish to be a little girl loved again—the security and everything I guess was taken for granted.

The main factor is that I don't feel that Bill respects my

feelings a whole lot—maybe he can't since he's so much older and more experienced—somehow, though, I'm not being my true self— all my inner feelings are suppressed, because he seems not too interested ever in hearing about anything that doesn't concern him or this type of life. Really, I'm not being fair to myself—I'm worrying too much and should let this black cloud blow over, then in a little while maybe the sun will shine.

Mom responded to my first letter noting that it was Sunday, Bastille Day, July 14, 1974. She was a stickler for dates and kept tidy records.

Dearest Annie,

Your letter was wonderfully welcome & I've re-read it many times. It's hard for me to comment on your life there for fear of sounding trite or trivial—but believe me I know and understand what each new bit of learning must mean to you. Everything I experienced at Wellington when it was primitive has a niche in my memory, and without those niches my sense of values would be totally altered. The country that surrounds you must be staggeringly beautiful; I hope to see it one day, though I have been to Flathead Lake & Glacier N.P., Vancouver, etc.

This is to be a brief letter as I'm busy with the usual city-fied and family duties. I'm about to go to market & then return Honey-Bee [my grandparents' 1957 Oldsmobile] to Manna. Dad will pick Didi up & take her to the usual Sunday there [at Manna and Pappy's house].

Tomorrow morning Dad & I have a confrontation with J. Fuller about some faulty goods & bills, & then I'm to pick up Millie Hoyt & Helen Arndt to go see Didi; I'll bring them here for lunch

& then take them to the shop. I have an early Tuesday meeting at Historic Denver & then will meet Rory Mentor at the shop. (We're hoping she'll help run it.) Then Jenny's coming for an 11:30 app't with Dr McKenna & I'll babysit. Jen still coughs & doesn't feel right.

And so it goes! I think I'd rather be milking goats & sleeping under "beavers & mountain lions."

Lovey, please don't go beyond your endurance; as you must realize you're not a match for a large, strong, experienced man.

I LOVE YOU—MOM

P.S. Do you need anything—drawing, fishing, camera?

Dad's first letter to me in mid-July was short but sweet. I could hear his voice as I read his note, and pictured him with a fly rod on the small stream near Boulder.

Annie Dearest,

Not only am I thinking of you I'm mainly wondering about exactly what you are doing almost on an hour-by-hour basis. Funny that it is a father's nature and perhaps a yearning to associate.

Life always seems to slow down without you here. That is normal. Youth always speeds the tempo of life. And that in itself says something. I am not as young as I was, except in spirit.

Yesterday I went fishing with Tony Taylor in his special spot near Boulder. You probably remember it. We fished hard and caught a few little ones but the focus was that I found clambering up the rocks and slipping down the banks has gotten harder. By the end of the day I was dog-tired. Now I'm recovered but what that little exercise says is that one must cherish youth but also rejoice that it is ephemeral.

The one really great thing we have is our minds—don't forget body —but most of all mankind had made his mark on this planet with his mind. Let us all work toward its betterment.

I love you with all my heart

Dad

Dad's gentle nudge toward the work of being a good, participating citizen was his way to guide me from a distance, and I appreciated his concern and involvement. I didn't entirely disagree, but was not planning to engage with the world as he suggested.

My view of the future of mankind was not hopeful. It seemed like our push toward progress in a modern world was destroying habitats and whole ecosystems, and the best thing to do as a human was to live off the land, using only natural materials. When the Foxfire books appeared in the early 1970s, they endorsed the simple lifestyle and contained a wealth of information about living off the grid, raising animals, making clothes, finding local foods, cooking, building structures, and much more. That series of three or four books became a homesteader's bible. My imperative was to learn all I could so that I could survive and thrive independent of society. Bill would teach me the skills I needed, and maybe someday I would be able to manage that lifestyle on my own, if I didn't stay with Bill forever.

In fact, Dad, Geof, and I had already been scouting for some property in Oregon with a fishing stream that we could enjoy in some shared arrangement. I resisted the idea that things would fall apart with Bill, but it seemed smart to have a plan B.

CHAPTER FIFTEEN

I wanted to share my new life with my sister. Jen would understand and support me without judgment, and just writing to her settled my spirit. I also included her husband in my notes; he was family, and it seemed like the normal thing to do. My first letter to them, dated July 11, recapped what I had described to Mom and Dad about chores, the animal antics, and the scenery, and went just under the surface to expose the issues I was facing in my new life.

Because I was anxious about my new role with Bill, I opened up to my sister and wrote that I had yet to experience the freedom that I had imagined. I mentioned that he was "never wrong about much of anything" and when I made a mistake, he made a "big deal" of it. Bill had scolded me the night before for not paying attention to careful storage and use of food after the deviled eggs incident. I explained that he was already cranky because of his shoulder injury from the day before.

Bill liked to tune in to certain talk shows during our meals and it often affected the tenor of the day. I wrote to my sister, "We listen to the radio which seems sort of ironic to be hearing ads about buy this, try that, this is your lucky day type of thing—but then the music is good sometimes." Those first unsettled feelings were so vivid, but I sensed that they would change over time, and I wanted to include a positive note, telling my sister that once I mastered the daily chores I would have the time to learn how to ride and do some beadwork. I signed off simply, "xxoo, Binks."

The next letter to my sister and brother-in-law in the third week of July was not as carefully crafted to disguise the frustration and unsteadiness I was feeling. I was looking to vent, and it seemed better to share that with my sister than my parents. My complaints about Bill were settling into some version of blame. I was sensing that I was already falling short of Bill's clearly stated expectations but was not exactly willing to admit that I'd had fair warning. Writing to my sister felt like I had someone listening as I hashed out my confusion over what Bill demanded, his lack of patience with me when I made mistakes, and my own self-criticism for "not watching and learning enough on my own."

But I had finally challenged myself to brave the river again, this time alone, and wanted to boast a little. That small success was surrounded by the doubts that seemed to persistently shade the background.

Swam across the river through the deep rapids yesterday, but is that a hairy situation! Just was swept down river so much that I thought I'd never reach the other side, and going back across was harder because I was expecting it and exerted too much strength I think, but now that I've done it, I really feel good, probably should do it every day as I'm letting myself get out of shape—there's good food, but mostly starches and I eat too much and Bill loves to eat cakes, cookies, and dinner at 8 or 9—so that's not so healthy, I think. Anyway, there's much to be done around here during the day, and that's not strenuous, just continuous. I'm already behind in my duties (such as the wood box is empty).

After a note about Bill's upcoming pack trip, my feelings about the choice I had made came to the surface:

> *The spirit for this kind of life is hard to come by, I've got the*
> *chance to live it, but so far am doing a poor job, perhaps I'm not*
> *ready, and am taking this all for granted.*
> *Anyway, take good care, love & miss you, Binks.*

Bill and I had been out with the horses a few times,
always bareback, and he had been urging me to do some
riding on my own. It made me nervous thinking about riding alone, but I was starting to gain some confidence from
our rides together and growing more at ease with Jude.

After an early supper somewhere in the second week of
July, Bill wanted to explore some of the territory across the
river, so we brought the horses out from the corral and put
their reins on. Bill cupped his hands for me to step in for a
boost onto Jude's back, then grabbed Jeremiah's mane and
tossed himself onto his back without effort.

As we started down the bank and into the river, my
body tensed; I had no way to control how Jude navigated
the slippery rocks and moving water. But she was calm and
steady and I realized that I had to relax, to trust her, and
to let her know that I had that confidence. Bill instructed
me to sit easily, and only try to guide her if I saw big rocks
or deep holes. The place where we forded was clear of those
obstacles, so my job was easy. On dry land we watched for
branches and unsteady ground.

By the time we got back to the ford in front of the cabin
late that afternoon, it was nearly dark and I was tired, but
feeling as though I had pushed some fear aside to simply
enjoy being on a horse.

A couple of days later, with chores behind me, I decided to take a ride on Jude by myself. She was in her own corral because the two-year-old stallion—Ahkee, her own colt—was trying to mount her when they were together. Bill was also trying to keep Rastes, the mule, and Jeremiah, the gelding, from getting into that mix of male horse hormones.

I grabbed a handful of grain and Jude's neck reins, and she came right over to me and stood while I put the reins over her head. There was a stump in front of the chicken coop, so I led her out to it and used it to help me climb onto her back, and then we headed out into the hay meadow.

The grasses had grown high in the three weeks since I'd arrived, and it was slightly breezy. As we walked across the meadow, I had the strange sensation of being in a boat, or floating, as the grasses rolled with the wind in green and silver waves. I had watched Bill as he and Ahkee or Jeremiah raced out across the meadow, mane and tail flowing behind and the fringe on Bill's buckskins a soft blur. It looked like a freedom I had never experienced. I squeezed my thighs tighter on Jude's flanks and urged her with a nudge; she broke into a trot, then a gallop, and we were flying!

The muscles in my legs and stomach were getting stronger, but I could only run with Jude for just so long before I wore out—I grew more fatigued riding than she did running. Soon, we slowed back to a walk.

Bill had seen us, and he came out on Ahkee, surprising me as he rode up behind us. "Hey Annie Gal," he said, grinning. "Looks like you're trying to outpace the wind out here."

As I grew stronger and began to adventure on my own, Bill was encouraged, and we grew a little easier around each other. I was pleased with my progress on the cooking front, managing the daily chores, and my measured adventures swimming and riding. He was usually helpful and even-tempered when he was instructing me, but he did not hide his frustration with me when I was not quick to pick up on a new task or if I wasted his time or supplies. Those first weeks were a mix of anxiety and the thrill of learning so many new skills. It was a balancing act, both physically and emotionally, and I was not all that practiced at living that way.

CHAPTER SIXTEEN

*M*y view of how things were going with Bill changed daily, depending on how competent I felt or whether Bill was in a good mood. In a letter to Mom and Dad postmarked July 20, I wrote that things were running smoother now.

Living around horses—and riding—was a new experience, and I was eager to give my parents a sense of the adventure that was unfolding for me. So I described my newfound relationship with riding in my letter, glad that I had something to share beyond a report of the round of chores. Then I included some casual notes about milking the goats, watching the kittens play and grow, and my improvements in the bread-baking and cooking departments. "It's a pleasant challenge and not too hard a duty," I told them. "Except Bill loves to eat, a lot—and keeping him fed and full is a big job."

I filled them in on Bill's planned trek, noting that he had said he might be gone as long as three weeks. Mentally preparing for that time alone, I mused about how I would spend that time thinking, doing beadwork, and canning the garden produce. I had no idea how to can, but I thought I'd figure it out.

Bill often had a project underway. I admired his workmanship and ability to create and hoped that I would find a way to carve out the time and space to do that for myself.

When he was busy with beadwork, ivory etching, or cutting and sewing a new buckskin shirt, he was calm and lighthearted. I enjoyed his creative focus and wanted to offer a glimpse of his craftsmanship to my parents:

> *Right now, it is a lazy day and Bill is finishing up some beading— he made a new pair of moccasins the other day and now is beading the design of a magpie on each top part of the toe— really beautiful —and when the beads glisten in the sun, wow! I have yet to finish fixing up a pair of moccasins I brought up here—those booted ones, and then I'll make a pair out of the softest buckskins made—those of a bull elk tanned in a brain solution and smoked—good lord they are beautiful!*

For some reason I then launched into a justification for Bill's arrogance and a note about his faults as I saw them— "(although he doesn't admit them) but I let things be and it's calmer that way—he can't stand a debate because he's usually right anyway."

By now I was figuring out that Bill was not going to listen to another point of view, at least not from me. There were times when I wanted to push back, but I was afraid of upending what was already a tentative agreement about my status as an apprentice, or whatever position I held. Even that was not really clear.

I asked whether my sister was feeling better and mentioned that I had not been sleeping soundly—mostly due to the mosquitoes and Chanticleer, the rooster, who woke me each morning at three o'clock. And of course, I added a note about Woink, who had a voracious appetite and was growing quickly. "Hope he doesn't decide to have me for his evening meal one of these days," I joked before closing, "I love you both always & forever, Annie xoxxo."

Midsummer days near the Canadian border were notably longer than what I was familiar with growing up in Denver; Bill's Val Halla sat a thousand miles north of my birthplace. Daylight broke early and lingered until well after nine o'clock in the evening. We usually had plenty of free time when we finished our afternoon round of chores, and Bill often wanted simply to relax or enjoy a small adventure. By the third week of July his shoulder had healed and he was eager to take another ride down the river, so we got the inner tubes from the barn and headed for the water.

The North Fork was not nearly as high with winter runoff as it had been the day I arrived, but it was still quite cold. About a mile downstream, we got out and carried our tubes to a series of beaver ponds at the far end of the meadow. Negotiating the ponds was like paddling through a maze; I was surprised at the vast realm the beavers had constructed. There was a huge beaver house in the uppermost pond, so we docked there and stood on the house to warm up a bit. The cold had penetrated my core and I welcomed the break. The air was permeated with a pungent odor from a cluster of herbaceous plants growing on the lodge, and we decided it was "beaver mint."

After we arrived home, I squirmed when I felt an engorged leech just below my buttock. Bill thought nothing of pulling it off, but I was truly embarrassed to have him touch me there in the daylight, especially to yank off a leech.

I was feeling self-conscious about my body and how Bill saw me. It was a constant undercurrent that contributed to the barrier of silence I put up when I wasn't sure how to react to Bill with intimacy. At night, when I had to pee, I didn't want to use the "thunder mug" under the bed, so I often waited until I was uncomfortable and then slipped away, hoping not to wake Bill, and went outside the shed door a few feet into the weeds. There was no way I was going to the outhouse in the dark. When I crawled back into bed afterward, I felt uneasy, afraid of disturbing Bill even further.

Sometimes I tried to nestle up to Bill in bed, but the touch was rarely returned. We slept together and had sex about every other night, and I was starting to wonder if I should be responding differently. Reaching a climax or even feeling pleasure seemed elusive, so I tried to compensate with pretense. Bill was already uncertain about my presence; the last thing I wanted to do was disappoint him sexually.

CHAPTER SEVENTEEN

*D*uring the hot spell in the third week of July, I wanted to find a way that I could cool off and get some exercise without swimming across the river. Beyond Joe and Flo's little cabin on the other side of the meadow there was a small brook that ran along the base of a slope, parallel to the meadow, and I thought that would be a perfect, private place to wash and refresh.

A few evenings earlier, Bill and I had forded that little stream on horseback to see if one of the only neighbors, a fellow named Paul, was at his cabin, somewhere beyond the top of the embankment. Bill had also mentioned that maybe he would give the kittens to Paul, and I liked that notion, since I was dreading the task of making them into mittens. Unfortunately, our mission was unsuccessful: Paul wasn't there.

After lunch on this day, while Bill was busy somewhere and I was on my own, I walked across the meadow toward the brook below the embankment where we had gone with the horses to look for Paul. Between the meadow and the brook there was a barrier of small shrubs, but I found the spot where we had led the horses through and felt the shade and cooler air flowing along with the water. It was not wider than about six or eight feet, and it was shallow, so I could easily sit on the bank and cool my feet, or maybe even strip down and bathe.

I sat down and took off my sneakers and socks. I was just stepping into the brook when I heard some rustling above me that was not the sound of wind, or the stream. I looked up to scan the bank, which was peppered with small trees and underbrush; the light was broken and dancing through the leaves. The movement of something about thirty feet away, up the bank and slightly to my right, caught my attention.

At first I took the large animal for a horse, with another following behind. *Maybe Bill is out with Jude and Rastes*, I thought. He could be going over to see if Paul was at his cabin, and I had not seen the kittens that day, so I was imagining a logical story to explain what I saw. Then the animal stopped, and the smaller one stopped, and the notion of "horse" disappeared as I noticed the hump on the bigger one's back—illuminated by the filtered light and shimmering a tawny gold.

The grizzly was slightly above me on the bank and she looked enormous—as big as a horse. Her cub was not much smaller, likely a two-year-old.

We looked at each other as I stood motionless in the shallow stream. She was beautiful and more impressive than any picture or mount in a museum display. My breath slowed and I ceased to be aware of my body; I just stood still, in awe. Her image was burning a place in my brain, and I wanted to stay in that moment. After several seconds, she turned her head to look forward and slowly continued on her path along the bank—right past me, just a few yards away.

As soon as the grizzly and her cub were out of sight, I hurried to dry my feet and put my socks and shoes back on so I could go tell Bill my news. Once I started to process what had just happened, I felt the rush of adrenaline—but it didn't feel like fear. It was more like thrill, or ecstasy. I ran all the way across the meadow to the cabin, not even feeling the heat. Bill was not inside, so I checked the barn and then the fishing cabin, where he sometimes went for a quiet afternoon nap. When I found him there, I told him about the grizzly and her cub, my heart still racing. He sat listening, then said, "Ha! Three bounds and you could have been lunch for that big Griz. Lucky for you she wasn't hungry."

In my journal, dated Friday, July 19, the same day I encountered the bear, I wrote, "What a feeling that was, to be face to face with a grizzly and know that she could have had me in her claws! Bill says that if I had turned and run while she was still standing facing me, she probably would have attacked—I guess I'm lucky she was sort of hidden and that I didn't realize what was going on."

As my impression of horse shifted to grizzly bear, I was thinking about how big she was, and how beautiful. Then I felt quiet and empty, peaceful, and there were no thoughts in my head. I had no control, as if I was witness to an event unfolding in a dream, but felt unbothered by that powerlessness. That strange calm was not something I had experienced before.

When the grizzly saw me, she stopped, and the cub took her cue, and for those few moments when our eyes met, I perceived it as a greeting. The cub and I acknowledged each other as well. I had read that you must *not* meet their eyes, as this was a sign of aggression. The safest behavior, it seemed, was to lower your eyes, speak calmly, and not turn to move away or make any rapid motions. But in the moment, none of that information entered my mind. She was just so beautiful; the filtered sun lit the long hair on her back and turned it to a silvery gold, and I wanted to capture that image of her and hold it close. The woods were rich with berries, so she probably wasn't hungry, but I was not even thinking about that. She must have understood that I was not a threat to her; if I had been anticipating seeing her, or had a gun or some other power over her, things might have evolved quite differently in those moments, but I did not sense any threat from her, and I didn't smell of fear. It was only after she and her cub were out of sight that I felt any surge of adrenaline, or thought about what had just happened.

I had also read that grizzly bears were unpredictable, but after this experience, I felt that had to do with humans having lost the ability to understand their fellow creatures on another level. The sensational stories and images of grizzlies as ferocious seemed like harmful information— more likely to result in unnecessary damage to a wild population than save human lives. I believed that a healthy dose of respect for, and a more intimate awareness of, other beings would open up a whole realm of communication and compassion.

Of course I was eager to write home about seeing the bears, but I didn't want Mom and Dad to worry, so I described a casual encounter without a hint of danger. I wrote to Dad and gave him a brief description of the scene, ending with, "Pretty exciting, isn't it?" I also mentioned the evening ride we had taken to find Paul, and a cow moose sighting on our way home past the beaver ponds. We were about one hundred yards away, and she never noticed us. I had seen moose in Yellowstone from a car, but was finding that it was much more vivid to encounter wildlife when you knew you were part of their realm.

In that same letter I wanted to reinforce the idea of finding a shared piece of land with Dad and Geof, "because I love this kind of life, but I'm feeling that I'm an imposition on Bill somehow, maybe that will wear off when I learn how to cook right! (so far, I've ruined a batch of beans, and two batches of rhubarb junk, and boy have I gotten grief)—oh well, live and learn, *n'est-ce pas?*"

On the outside of that envelope, I added a note about the current events that we heard on our radio, since Dad was a news hound and interested in world affairs. "Now the Turks and Greeks are at war, and my thinking is that soon we will be in a war such as world war III—as there are so many not at ease with themselves or their country, not to mention other nations. Anyway . . . it's a great threat so we must be wary."

In late July, Dad started a letter to me and then finished a couple of days later, after he had received my letter to him about the grizzlies.

Saturday July 27

My Dearest Annie—

In my mind I've started a letter to you at least a hundred times in the last two days. And still, I'm at a loss as to where to begin. What you have to say, and wonderfully so! is so far removed from my relatively insignificant involvements—i.e. by your standards.

Monday July 29

Annie my dear one

I am wondering what you are doing as I write. Indeed, I wonder a great deal. Your frequent letters are a cause for joy and comfort and interest always. The bear episode sounded hairy. Keep a very discreet distance. They are treacherous animals.

The shop has sort of become my office and home away from home. And believe it or not we've actually sold a few things . . . And our shipment from Italy is due to arrive in a week or two—phew! I'd better get moving because as of now there wouldn't be space to put all the stuff.

The judiciary hearings on impeachment are historic and fascinating. They're all being T.V.ed and much of what is said is quite moving. It's sort of like act two of a good mystery. It seems to be a consensus that Nixon will be impeached by the House of Representatives and likely be convicted by the Senate. If so and if it is televised it will be one of the great dramas in our history. For once I think he should be convicted since to me the evidence is clear that he has obstructed justice, as well as directed criminal activities within the government and failed to uphold the laws.

Hope you will begin to paint and draw to capture for me some of those scenes about you.

Ever lovingly, Dad

The political news arriving in bits through Dad or the radio and entering our realm of grizzly bears and big rivers was an odd juxtaposition. I did find peace in the focus on the world just outside our door, consistent with Bill's tenth premise about keeping the larger world out of our view, but the current world events always seeped in and Bill had his opinions about all of it. I often wondered why he listened to the radio, given how it sent distracting waves through his Val Halla paradise.

We listened to the news about Nixon and the almost

certain impeachment, and as disconnected as I was from the politics of our country, the news was encouraging. I had read and heard enough to believe that Nixon was a crook, and I also had to weigh what I heard on the right-wing talk radio program with whatever Bill gleaned and professed. He seemed to absorb whatever diatribe they spouted as if it were the truth. Sometimes his distorted view influenced my own, including some of what I shared with my dad. Bill didn't disagree that Nixon was dishonest, and a schemer. He was keen to praise Kissinger, however, believing that his politics lined up with the philosophy of Ayn Rand as expressed in *Atlas Shrugged*. Rand's 1956 novel laid out the theme that the capitalist structure of American wealth was derived from poor laborers and that complete control and ownership of resources and intellectual property was obtained by threat, pointing to an inevitable dictatorship. Bill often referred to *Atlas Shrugged* as his dystopian philosophy, and he felt that Rand's endorsement of individualism and self-support was the only way to achieve freedom from the oppression of socialism. Much of Rand's philosophy did seem to hold true when Bill described it, but its basic premise also emanated hatred and fear.

I did not have the knowledge to rebut these concepts, so I adopted the parts that seemed to make sense. During the time I lived with Bill, my view shifted to accommodate some of his anger, in spite of the discomfort I felt when I repeated his words in my letters.

When Dad shared his political views he was thoughtful, and a gentleman, and I trusted his opinion, so I enjoyed our back-and-forth in letters.

"Dear Dad," I wrote on August 1, "Looks like ol' pres ain't going to make it after all his evasive tactics eh what? Well, it's about time, the dumb jerk ought to be hanged anyway, but then if congress puts Ford in his place, ugh! Bill thinks Kissinger might reverse the speed of our destruction and perhaps straighten up a mixed up, mechanized, down-the-hole country. I really haven't an opinion, I only know that our government is going to fold, and when it does, the country doesn't have the spirit to pick itself up again."

Along with those thoughts I added that I was still hopeful about the property we had seen in Oregon, thinking a gentle nudge in that direction would keep that dream alive. I wrote, "Now I'm aiming at a high goal, to be able to live this life alone, so I've got to get good at hunting, wintering, sewing. I've really got to toughen up, otherwise Bill might boot me, as I've not been using my time very wisely, but I'm learning."

Thinking of Dad made me a little blue. I saw him as both solid and somehow vulnerable, and I wanted to let him know how much I cared for him. After a short, slightly unfair note about his participation in the "mechanical, bill-paying, money system," I told him that I was happy that he had the freedom to enjoy his life, saying, "I've never heard you complain that you're bored or anything—so you are a very, very lucky, one of a kind, Dad, and being blind as I am, could never see it before. Much love, take good care, Annie."

Dad's grace and positive outlook boosted my spirits like a tonic. He was a fair judge to all, and his views gave me some perspective against Bill's condemnation of people, or even whole societies. Even though I was absorbing and reciting many of Bill's tenets, I always had my father's measured and thoughtful position to keep me balanced.

✕

CHAPTER EIGHTEEN

ournal entry, Friday July 26, 1974

> *Today was learn to can whortleberry day, and Bill thought I was so
> stupid that he left for town in an awful hurry. Well, he never
> explained it all at once, just in pieces, so I mixed the pieces up by
> accident and asked crazy questions. He's getting sort of impatient
> with me, because he thinks I'm taking this life for granted—what
> am I supposed to say—Oh, Bill, I think you're so wonderful I
> absolutely cherish everything you've done here!? Is that what I
> should do? . . . he tells me that I ought not to use my chores as an
> excuse for not doing things I can be proud of . . .*

The tension with Bill was shifting to be a more low-grade
constant as my initial grace period ended. I didn't argue
with him, or try to defend my mistakes; I knew they were
costly and unacceptable. This was not an apprenticeship
with a kindly instructor. But I was also used to having
more leeway, so I quietly grumbled and made excuses for
myself, especially in my journal.

After a month with Bill, I was trying hard to make
sense of my place in his world and was not yet settling into
a comfortable position. In a long letter I wrote to Mom and
Dad on July 28, I was alone again for a day or two because
Bill had gone down to Kalispell for more supplies for his

pack trip. I wrote to my parents that it was nice to be on my own, and not "under his thumb, or watchful eye."

Much of my letter circled around the same issues I had already expressed about Bill's demands, my efforts to keep a clean cabin, prepare food, and manage the chores, and my frustration about not feeling adequate or appreciated. I admitted that Bill was "hard as hell to get along with." But the homesteading lifestyle suited me, I told them, though it would be even more ideal with friends and family to share and enjoy it with. "I guess you're getting that it's not all so happy," I wrote. "Beautiful and free, yes, but it would be even more free and alive were I with ones I love." I added that I had always taken so much for granted but now had a new perspective on the hard work it takes to build any kind of decent life, wherever that may be.

I wanted to be clear that I was grateful, but it would be a long time before I would be able to "earn my keep" independent of my parents. That thought included the notion that if and when I returned home, it meant getting a job— probably cleaning houses, or maybe as a farmhand—until my brother and Dad and I could find a piece of property where I could set up my own homestead.

I wrote that I was wary of becoming the "wage-earning slave" that Bill was constantly condemning. As I tried to work out my conflict on paper, I admitted that I had "everything I need and want, except for a good feeling inside. Why does that part have to be missing? Maybe it will just take time to work out—maybe I'm just homesick and have to blab, maybe I'm too damned concerned over Annie's little problems, when I think of what's going on in the world, that makes me pretty small."

At the end of the letter, I urged Mom and Dad to see that the world as they enjoyed it was not sustainable. The tendency of those with means to accumulate material goods, throwing them away only to replace them with more and newer models and styles, was entirely wrong—tapping resources at the expense of the environment, abusing the land and people in faraway places for their raw materials, and passing on the expense and sorrow of terribly compromised environments to future generations, especially in the backyards of the poor and on the backs of the laborers. These were my own long-held thoughts which, unlike Bill's screed that seemed to hold so much anger, had emerged out of my fear and intuition.

Still, our negative views of the future did line up in many ways. "The world isn't going to last much longer anyway," I warned my parents. "With wars, shortages, and depressions at hand, I don't see how we can survive, knowing the white man is too poor a creature to organize and pull his race together to try and solve things—everyone is too lazy, always says—'Oh, it'll never happen to us.' I suggest you rip out your roses and plant a huge vegetable garden—chuck all your appliances, and get two goats, and be very conscientious about waste, seriously, and pollution, for god sakes trade in those two gas hogs and get a horse!!! Really, we are so uncareful, always throwing away, etc, etc."

Writing to Mom and Dad helped me process my confusion. They were concerned, and understood that I was trying to assert myself in my adopted life, and were forgiving of my fits and starts. Their letters from home provided an emotional sanctuary, even though I was trying to set myself apart from that culture. Mom and Dad often commented about the comfort of their country club lifestyle, acknowledging that it was set against my wilderness-world backdrop of hauling water and adventures with animals; they seemed to be able to hold a clearer perspective than I could of both of our chosen ways of life. Our relationship was growing deeper and more valuable through letters, although I was not as generously accepting of the life they had established and kept up my effort to make them see the world differently. Mom had been my model and instructor about being less wasteful, so I felt that she should better understand my position; she had a place in her heart for the cabin life, and I was grateful to share that with her. However, Mom was entirely honest and did not make excuses for the lifestyle she enjoyed, and I did appreciate that she was so sturdy in that regard. In her direct way, she engaged with me and my experience, sending occasional books and articles, including a book titled *A Day No Pigs Would Die*, since I had told them so much about Woink and she was growing fond of him from a distance.

I smiled when Mom sent a short, newsy letter at the beginning of August with bits and pieces about the day-to-day at home. She mentioned that the neighbors were there swimming, with Josie sitting and watching from the kitchen door. She shared that they had "three sizeable" dinner parties coming up, and that they'd enjoyed a nice weekend fishing with friends on the South Platte river at their cabin above Denver. Even a brief note from Mom was welcome, and I didn't mind that she occasionally wrote to tell me that she didn't have much to say.

Sometimes she expressed herself as if we were talking on the phone. On Sunday, July 28, she wrote:

Dear love, I'm going to flunk on letter writing at this point in time. I've had so many interruptions that it's impossible to concentrate. A swimming pool is dubbed an attractive nuisance, though we've enjoyed those who have come . . . In some ways I wish I were milking goats, feeding Woink—riding bareback—merely living primitively, though I do relish in the creature comforts.

I (we) read your letters over & over and of course I'm keeping them because they're in the nature of a diary. There are many personal questions I would like to have answered—but I won't invade your privacy, nor do I think you would want that recorded. However, being a mother???

I've talked with Don at the Gallery & Cini came over yesterday. The Carsons are fishing in Wyo.

Dad has left to pick up Didi for Manna's & Pap's & I'll leave for the P.O.

I love you so much, Mom

On July 31, in response to her "personal question," knowing that it was an inquiry about whether I was involved with Bill sexually, I wrote,

Dear Mom,

My guess is that you're wondering about the sex deal, well yes, Bill and I have indulged—that is to say, he's indulged, I haven't quite got the hang of it yet, and so it's not exactly my favorite pastime, but now that my period's come on schedule, there's no fear of pregnancy and so there's no more hang-ups in my head. Well, actually there must be if the enjoyment is lacking. But really, it's been pounded into my head from a crooked society that sex is deplorable and perverted and it comes across as a twisted nighttime activity instead of the beautiful thing given and shared by two people. Now that I can look at it as something not to be feared, things will go better. Bill loves it, but he must be able to tell that I'm as cold as ice.

Maybe I was expecting to be in love to make love, that's on its

way later I hope, because to love the one you're with always eases life, no? He knows that time will have to take its course with me, and when I don't want it, I tell him, and he knows not to push the matter, so there are no ill feelings. And I do like him, because he talks so much about things he's always thought and known and seen. I know very little and am not the wise careful one with the insight, but foresight, hindsight—he is opening my eyes to his thought, which is in one direction, but the right one.

Love you, don't fret, life's to live, Annie

Naturally, Mom was curious about my relationship with Bill, and I wanted to paint my emotional landscape for her: the missing elements of joy and easiness. She had a way, without knowing all the details, of seeing into my heart. When I wrote to her that I thought the way the media depicted sex made it seem "dirty," it was a disguise for the confused tangle of sex and sorrow I wanted to forget. In some way, I was trying to share that with her, but I framed it as blame for society at large. In truth, my exposure to *Playboy* magazines from a young age, the advances of neighborhood boys that were not in the least bit romantic, and my relationship with my brother-in-law had colored my early views of sex. And the adults in my world did not exhibit much in the way of love openly, so I didn't have the most positive models for sex and partnerships. Still, in spite of the lack of tenderness and intimacy with Bill, I believed that romance and the ideal of true love had to exist, and that I would find it.

It's just that the potential did not seem to be anywhere in sight with Bill. I thought about how he'd approached me one day when I was practicing throwing the tomahawk at two turns into the stump. He said that if I threw the tomahawk three times in a row at two turns (or rotations), he'd "carry me inside and seduce me."

I processed that quickly and quietly; he had never approached me in that way before. Did that mean he was starting to feel a deeper interest in me? It made me nervous, and I almost expected not to be able to throw the tomahawk after that, like the pressure of the game in competition, but I did. He laughed and tossed me onto his shoulder and carried me inside and up the narrow stairs, and I flashed on the image of a caveman carrying a woman into the dark of his cave. *Oh dear*, I thought; it was the middle of the day, and I wasn't prepared. I would have wanted time to clean up and feel easy or ready.

We did have sex, but it was frustrating to have the enjoyment of that rare spontaneous occasion be so overwhelmed by my nervous inner dialogue.

Mom wrote back right away to share her insight and understanding. On Monday, August 5, she wrote:

Dearest Annie,

Thank you, love, for your letter. I should have tried to prepare you emotionally, as well as bodily, for sex; somehow, we never took the time to be alone to discuss such matters. Sex is such a personal and individual thing that probably we wouldn't have had a satisfactory talk anyway. Even though I told you that I thought intercourse was inevitable, I hoped that it would come slowly, gently, understandingly & with compassion.

Actually, in most cases, it takes a lot of time and experience to achieve a satisfying union, and you are so young and inexperienced and I had hoped that he would teach you how satisfying, if not beautiful, the relationship can be. I'm sorry that this "crooked society" has given you the impression that sex is "deplorable"; it can seem so when you read or hear of sex-related crimes or see movies or T.V. that make it seem overly carnal or twisted. But, dear girl, desire & passion have been around forever, and you will adjust and enjoy it when the right time and/or person comes your way. I truly feel for you—but don't worry, if you feel you are in safe hands.

As usual I must cut this short—now to make supper.

Questions:

- How do you get & send mail?
- Did you get the books I sent?
- Can I send you anything?
- Do you have radio communication, two-way or what?

Know that I love you so very much. Mom

Please don't swim the river alone—but of course I have no control over that and you well know the power of water.

Opening up with Mom about sex and relationships strengthened our bond. Her thoughts about the time it would take to establish trust and deeper feelings were measured, and I appreciated her experience. The involvement with my brother-in-law had informed my notion about how sex could determine a connection between two people, and I wanted something different, something honest and caring.

I couldn't share that with Mom, of course. That situation had been so wrong, and bereft of any feelings of love, ultimately, and I was relieved that it was in my past. But now I just felt hollow, and I wasn't sure if there was a way to change the landscape of my relationship with Bill.

CHAPTER NINETEEN

*T*he letters I sent home often crossed in the mail with my parents', and my letter to Mom and Dad at the end of July that was filled with confusion and upset was landing in their box just as I'd settled into a different emotional place. My thoughts and moods would shift and grow lighter when I simply busied myself weeding the garden or managed to wash a pile of dirty clothes. Small accomplishments felt almost as productive as learning the more in-depth skills. On mail days, when I opened letters from my parents, I felt a disconnect with their responses to my thoughts from days ago, and I'd have to try to remember what I had shared with them. Sometimes I regretted writing when I was anxious or upset, since it worried them more than I ever considered in the moment.

When Mom wrote on Wednesday, August 7, she addressed my letter from the end of July.

Dearest Annie—

Your letter yesterday sounded somewhat desperate—confused, frustrated & lonely. Bill seems to be unreasonable & demanding, & he's using you, though you more or less asked for it. I think it's time for you to think about coming home to re-evaluate, for certainly there's no future for you where you are and an alternative way must be found, hopefully with our help and guidance, love and

*understanding. However when you do come home, I don't want you
to try to alter our lifestyle. What is right for you and/or Bill is not
necessarily right for all of mankind—in fact it's physically
impossible at this point in time. As long as Dad & I are together &
live in this house our pattern is pretty much established & I don't
want you to try to pull it apart. I, too, loved the Oregon property
and would like to have it as a way of life a bit at a time; you are
young and can make it your way but, as I said, we are established
and have earned and enjoy our "creature comforts." I wouldn't
dream of pulling out the roses because beauty—when it can be
found, is what life is all about. It's not possible to get rid of the cars
and park a horse at the tennis court or the Safeway. If we die of
starvation or pesticides or pollution or revolution, then it's timely
that we do so.*

*Dad said he wrote to you that he's going to continue to look for
the right kind of land. I'm hoping that if you do come home, and as
an interim occupation, that you could work for Salty & Bob [my
godmother's family] or help with her mother's ranch. There's lots to
be done & they have very little help & lots of peace.*

I love you so very much, Mom

No doubt Mom worried and felt confused about my wide
emotional swings as I tried to fit into Bill's world. She responded directly to whatever concerns or adventures I
shared and was keenly aware of my internal struggle. The
angst-filled missive she'd responded to here had begged for
answers and support, even though I rejected the notion of
going home. My harsh words reflected reaction more than
careful consideration, as if it was a way to establish a distance from them and ignore the questionable choices I had
made.

Every day with Bill, I waged a battle in my mind about whether I could manage to stay, or if my struggle meant I was feeling defeated and afraid to admit my failure. If I continued to openly reject the safety and comfort of home, I thought, maybe the doubts about this world I stepped into with Bill would fade.

August 8 was a chilly day, and the drizzle seemed ready to turn to snow—notable weather after the recent hot spell, which had lasted for three weeks. It was also the day that Nixon resigned, and addressed the nation with his resignation speech. We listened to him on the radio, and I knew my parents would be watching it on TV. I wrote to them that evening and, from my naïve vantage point, weighed in with a few comments about Henry Kissinger's strengths and the weakness of the Congress in handling the Nixon debacle.

Most of my letter, however, was in response to a note that Cini had sent to me after going over to talk to my parents a week or two earlier. Mom and Dad had invited her over because they were worried about me and thought she could shed some light on my situation or maybe influence me, as a friend, to rethink my future. I interpreted their action as an attempt to urge me to come home and look for different options, and to protect me, as if I were a child. Cini mentioned that Mom and Dad knew it would be hard, if not unhappy, for me to be home. I agreed with that, and I tried to convince all of them that I was setting my own course, extreme as it might seem.

I wrote that although the initial few weeks had seemed so uncertain, they were behind me. I reassured them that "the chores are a joy now, and I'm learning about how to use my time well. The animals are my friends, and the whole atmosphere is calmer. Each day I just love and it's odd that I've not been bored, but how can I be? There's always something to do."

Bill had been talking about the winter as a beautiful time—how the vast, white wilderness settled his spirit. I told my parents that he was enjoying my company now and expecting me to stay through the winter, and I hoped I would be able to experience that world in its cloaked white glory. But he hadn't hesitated to add that it was harsh, and that we would be much more at the mercy of nature outside in the cold and snow. I pictured the warmth of the woodstove, and a pot of soup simmering. I also understood the reality and risks of trying to manage daily life in the winter weather, including long, dark nights and going outside to pee, and it made me nervous about my ability to cope.

Most of all I dreaded having to make mittens out of the kittens. We had shared this idea with a neighbor who stopped by one day; apparently that news had traveled, and Bill had gotten wind of the ensuing gossip from Joe and Flo. Making mittens out of barn cats was not a normal practice, and the neighbors had reacted with alarm. Bill seemed to enjoy getting a rise out of people and worked to enhance his image as a wild man, an outsider. He had lots to say about how people talked about him. I mentioned the gossip chain to my parents and how Bill viewed the neighbors, which was not entirely friendly.

Even as I was trying to convince my parents that life with Bill was improving, I wrote that I was sure he was often thinking of Helen. I knew he had loved her truly, and I sensed he still missed her. He had once told me that Helen just couldn't believe in the paradise he'd built for them at Val Halla, but I imagined that she wasn't solely to blame for leaving. My doubts about Bill's feelings for me were a constant, and I couldn't ever picture him loving me truly in the way I knew he'd loved Helen.

CHAPTER TWENTY

*A*s August settled in, Bill readied his supplies and gear for his pack trip. He spent time showing me how to take care of the garden while he was gone, and some other small tasks. I would not need to do any canning; what a relief.

I watched as Bill headed out on his trek across the high peaks riding Jeremiah, with Rastes, loaded with his gear, and Ahkee, whom he was bringing along to train, trailing behind him. It would be a nice break to not cook for him or worry about being scrutinized about my activity and production for a while.

The chores helped break up the hours, but I struggled with all the unstructured time. In those first couple of days alone, I ate differently, and more than I would have if Bill had been there, and I couldn't seem to get started on much of anything creative. While I had the piano to myself, I slowly worked on the first part of Rachmaninoff's "Prelude in C-sharp minor," an intense, engaging piece of music to listen to and to play with large major and minor chords requiring both hands to weave together and pound intently. Years' worth of dust and disorganization meant there was always some cleaning to do, and I felt gratified if the cabin was tidy. I took walks, tended to chores, wrote, read, and found small distractions to fill the time.

The day after Bill left, I was surprised to see Ahkee

near the barn. The young stallion was supposed to be with Bill, but here he was, no doubt to be near Jude, who was now in heat and was being kept in the barn. I kept an eye out for Bill to return for Ahkee, but after a day I decided he must have figured that Ahkee would head for home and was safe. The stallion stood stubbornly outside of Jude's stall, but I was not about to let her out; I was sure he would mount her if I did.

The next day, when I saw that Joe and Flo had just arrived at their little one-room cabin across the meadow, everything about the day brightened. I was eager for company, but I also wanted to appear capable and in charge. Maybe that was the incentive for deciding to ride Ahkee over to see them.

Ahkee was Bill's special horse. He was chestnut-colored and sleek, and stood about fifteen hands high. At only two years old, he was not yet entirely broken and Bill was still working with him, training him to neck rein and not rear or buck. He was almost there, but he wasn't there yet.

There was no good reason for me to even consider riding Ahkee, but reason didn't enter my mind as I headed for the barn to retrieve him.

I had tried to swing up onto Jude's back a few times, as I'd seen Bill do, but for my small frame it was more like a circus move that I'd need to train for. Plus, the weight I'd put on had made me less agile. Without really thinking through how I would get Ahkee to take me across the meadow without a halter, not to mention wait for me to visit and then ride home, I walked up to him, grabbed his mane, and flew my leg up in the air like I had seen Bill do—and the rest of me followed up onto his back.

This surprised me more than it did Ahkee, though I'm sure it wasn't what he had in mind. As soon as I was on his back, he bolted and launched into a full run. I grabbed his mane and gripped his flanks with my thighs as hard as I could, clinging to him—there was no other choice.

He cleared the barn and made a hard, tight turn around the corner toward the river, and then a second right turn at the corner of the barn so we were racing along the top of the river bank. He ran between two trees so close together that I had to bring my legs up and behind me onto his back. This took away my ability to grip with my legs, but I reached around his neck and stayed on out of sheer will and fear for my life.

Just past the cabin, Ahkee made another right turn between the cabin and the pig pen, brushing close to another tree, then sped around the end of the cabin between the garden and the root house before finally running full speed to the front of the barn, where he did one of those classic cartoon dead stops, just like the Roadrunner. I slid off his back, amazed that we were back where we started after such a brief but memorable ride.

Eager to tell them what had just happened, I ran across the meadow to Joe and Flo's cabin. When I did, Joe dropped his usual joyous smile and looked alarmed. He nearly scolded me as he told me how he had lost his leg from a similar incident, riding a horse with only a belt around its neck and getting caught in the belt when the horse threw him. His ankle was so badly broken that after five years and multiple surgeries the leg had to come off below the knee. I was sorry to upset Joe. Flo showed her concern and also gave me what-for. *Don't be so foolish! You don't know how powerful that horse is, and he's young.* I was not about to tell Bill.

In my journal I wrote about my short, exciting ride, adding a poem I'd composed for Bill. The lines go back and forth between Ahkee and a sparrow hawk whose cry was the piercing "ah-h-ke-e-e!!" that Bill named him after.

"Bill is awfully fond of Ahkee, the young 'puppy,'" I wrote. "Oh he's a sweet one—This poem was written for Bill when he was gone on his mountain trek . . ."

Ahkee! The piercing cry
From blood red peaks beneath twilight sky
Ahkee! Again he calls
A winging hawk, the sparrow stalls—

Silent. Erect he stays, awaits the cry.
The stallion's gaze cast is fiercely proud
No thoughts of fear do this soul crowd.

Ahkee! Now folded wings
A dive, a sweep, a blow that brings him prey.
Ahkee! He'll laugh
A battle won with strength but half

Intent. Black tail and mane alone do dare,
by moon on wane to show a slight unrest

Ahkee! With prize he'll seek his nest.
Who-oo. The night is come to cast its dream.
Unseen freedom finds proudest spirit wild and
free as birds of prey in flight. Ahkee!

Because of Ahkee, Bill did in fact cut his trip short; he returned to Val Halla after just five or six days. I was glad for his return, because in spite of a certain tension that persisted, we'd grown closer as partners, or at least workmates, through our routines and interactions. We often worked together in the garden, weeding, and Bill would boast about his special gardening knowledge, including how he could grow head-size "rooty beggars." Or I might be cooking something, and he would sample it and tell me that it tasted great. When I was cutting onions one day for dinner and he saw that I was clumsy with a small knife, he put the big chef's knife in my hands and showed me how to efficiently use the knife in a rocking motion to quickly dice or mince. It felt good to do things the right way.

A couple of days after he got home, Bill suggested that we take the truck for berry picking, since we might come back with more than we wanted to carry on horseback. There was a patch of huckleberries up the embankment toward Paul's place, near where I had seen the grizzly and her cub, and he was eager to pick them before the bears got to them. (Huckleberries are similar to blueberries, just a bit more on the tart side, and firmer.)

We drove south about a mile on the main road and pulled into Paul's dirt road, heading back north. The large patch we were looking for was located toward the top of the embankment above our meadow, on a gentle, rocky knoll.

Huckleberries are low-growing, like low-bush blueberries, so we squatted at the edge of the abundance with our buckets and started picking. After a couple of hours, my hands were growing numb, and I laughed when I tried to pick my purple thumb more than once.

As the mosquitos grew thick at dusk, it was time to go. We left with almost seven gallons of berries! It was late when we got home, so we just had corn flakes for dinner before falling into bed.

There were several tasks that I could not do entirely on my own yet, including canning. My first experience with the whortleberries (vernacular for huckle and blueberries), and Bill's upset with my inability to grasp the process from the get-go, had left me feeling edgy. But the peas were ripe and ready to process, so it was time to learn.

Bill had to tell me, step by step, how to can the peas. It was an intense experience that I shared in a letter to my sister-in-law, Sherry. On August 12, I wrote:

The garden is growing like a demon, and I've canned up so many peas it's incredible—but to can them, there's the prerequisite of picking and shelling—I'm in a pea-picker's paradise, or prison, whichever, but I'm up to my ears with them. Also canned up 77 qts. of cherries in two days!! Spending 8-9 hours the first day next to a roaring fire, brother! And you've got to watch the temp. gauge so it never goes beyond a certain amount of pressure—peas take 40 min.—but I usually wash dishes so I can keep an eagle's watch on that gauge.

It was my first big canning chore since that negative whortleberry episode. I was nervous just thinking about it after Bill warned me that peas had to stay at the same temperature and not vary more than one or two degrees because they had none of the acids of fruits that prevent bacteria from growing, and the cooking time was specific so that the peas were neither undercooked nor overcooked.

After I picked and shelled an infinite number of peas, I loaded up the wood stove to try to bring it to a steady, even temperature. Then I sterilized the pint jars—avoiding touching any rims or sealing lids, since that could contaminate them with bacteria.

Well, something went wrong along the way. A few weeks later I discovered the lids of the canned peas were bloated and unsealed and the peas had grown cloudy: they were infected with botulism. I felt awful and dreaded telling Bill the bad news. I couldn't feed them to Woink or the chickens; it was a total waste of about forty pints of peas.

All the time, labor, and loss of food was serious, and Bill was furious. There was nothing I could do to replace the peas, and it compounded my feelings of failure to ruin food that he had grown and relied on having for the winter ahead.

That incident remained a dark cloud, even though we never mentioned it again.

Almost everything new was a challenge, and the anticipation of whether or not I could manage the rigorous lifestyle built up like clouds of doubt. A few days after Bill arrived back from his trip, he came in as I was finishing the dishes and told me that one of the hens was not looking good. She would not be long for the world, he said; she was riddled with lice and scrawny, and she never laid eggs. It was time to butcher her before she made the other hens sick.

My stomach churned with that nervous going-to-the-doctor feeling.

"Today you get to kill a chicken. I want to watch how you handle a hatchet," he said matter-of-factly.

"Right now?" I asked.

"No better time," he answered.

He told me to fill a big pot of water to boil where I would plunge her body to loosen the feathers for easier plucking. Then I followed him outside.

If I never have to kill a chicken again, it will be too

soon. It was certainly part of raising animals for food, and that must have been my mantra so that I could do the deed. Still, I dreaded that job.

When I went to catch her, Bill stood by and watched. She must have been terrified, poor thing, and the more I chased her, the more frantic she became. Bill laughed at the sight but I was near tears. It was awful. I was hoping that maybe she could escape.

The chase lasted much longer in my head than in reality, and I finally caught her in a corner of the yard. Then Bill instructed me to hold her by her feet and put her head on the stump that sat between the cabin and the pig/chicken pen.

She was struggling and panicked, and so was I. Bill handed the hatchet to me and I took a swing without really preparing or thinking through what had to happen, because I did not want to kill her. I swung but looked away—missing her neck and chopping into her shoulder. She fell off the stump and started running around the yard.

Bill just stood there with his arms crossed and told me to hurry and catch her again, and swing with my eyes open this time!

I did, determined and focused, and on the second attempt I cut her head off. When I tossed her still-struggling body, she actually did a few headless dance steps before growing still. My eyes must have been so wide; it was like an unsettling dream you can't wake from.

I carried her in and put her into the boiling water for a few seconds, then plunged her into cold water so her muscles wouldn't toughen or cook. Plucking seemed to take forever; I sat there in the yard and plucked and plucked, glad that the killing part was over and wondering if we really needed chickens to survive. Then I gutted her. Bill talked me through it, but since it was my lesson, I did all of the work. I dressed her out, cut her up, and put her in a big pot to cook. By the end, I felt a little victorious; I had just made another step toward learning something about survival.

Since we had noodles, I thought that chicken tetrazzini would be a good dish to cook. I always loved Mom's creamy and rich tarragon-infused specialty. The chicken simmered for a good long time, and the meat should have been done and tender after an hour or so, but it didn't seem to be getting to that tender stage, so I let it stew for at least another hour. After that second hour the meat was certainly "done," but nowhere near tender; it was closer to the texture of rubber than it was to stewed meat. I forged ahead and came up with some kind of creamy herbed sauce, and I think we enjoyed the dish, even if we did have to chew like crazy. At the time I thought I hadn't cooked her long enough, but now I figure her muscles toughened with the panic and rush of adrenaline.

On August 15, I got another letter from Mom that addressed my strident but mixed messages.

Dearest Annie

Some of your letters have been way up—and some way down, so it's I who am confused as to what state you're in—emotionally & physically. Certainly, we don't want you to come home to be our "12 year old" or "baby." You've been away from home a lot—camp, France & E.W. [Emma Willard School] & I agree that to compromise our philosophies and ways of life would be virtually impossible at home; you have no goal, purpose, occupation or even

*pleasure here. This is not meant to be criticism—simply a fact. If
what you're doing is meaningful & satisfying to you, great! but
certainly it can't be a forever situation for a girl with a fine brain
and artistic talent. You also have the ability, background, &
education to offer something in this world other than to yourself. I
honor what you're doing but I look at it as an interim way of
seeking peace and finding yourself. Most people never really find
themselves, and I can't say that I have. However I treasure most of
the experiences & privileges that have come my way, including Dad
& my four blessed children & their families.*

    I love you so very much my dearest Annie.

    Mom

Mom's strong, clear message resonated with me, and I felt
ashamed of both my lack of certainty and show of distress. It
was hard on my parents to know that I was unhappy, or
afraid, and dealing with a man who was not entirely welcoming. I resolved to try to be more positive, and just engage in
the new life I had chosen without complaint.

When I wrote home August 16, I recapped but made
light of my misadventure with Ahkee. I knew I'd been
lucky, and that my hanging-on instinct had compensated
for my lack of experience. It was the kind of risk Bill had
warned me about, I just hadn't conceived of the danger of
getting on a horse alone—the razor-thin line between life
and death had not been apparent to me. But Joe and Flo's
stern admonitions stressed that I was not as skilled with
horses as I thought, and that a simple act could mean trouble, or worse.

CHAPTER TWENTY-ONE

*9*n answer to Mom's concerns and thoughts, the next letter I sent to my parents, postmarked August 19, continued with the notion of coming home or not. I told Mom
and Dad that I was feeling productive, learning, and growing, but that "somehow, I know, too, that this will probably
not be a forever thing—because I don't love the man, and
maybe sentiments will change." The rest of the letter ram-
bled through descriptions of our daily life, as usual.

Before I signed off, I mentioned that Bill's friend Ken
and a girl who I described as a "Berkeley babe" had just
arrived.

Ken Iddins looked wild with his long, dark hair and
beard, but his eyes sparkled and softened the scragginess.
He was one of the gentler souls I'd ever met. Ken and Bill
had known each other for years; they'd met in the service at
an intense time in their lives. Ken was still stationed in
Alaska in some kind of communications and reconnaissance
branch of the civil service. His post was on a tiny island
about as far out from the continent and as close to Russia
as you could get—a cold-war post, no doubt. He had driven
down through Olympia, Washington, to visit family, then
headed for Val Halla.

When Ken stepped out of his truck, he and Bill hugged
hard, then proceeded to joke as only old friends can do. Ken
produced a huge salmon, at least twenty-four inches long,

that he'd brought from Washington, kept on ice in a large cooler. Bill accused him of having stolen it from an Eskimo, and they broke into a belly laugh. Of course, he'd caught it himself; Ken was as much a survivor as Bill. He had lived in extremely harsh conditions in Alaska, and spent time hunting caribou, fishing, and trekking alone through vast wilderness. He was a creative sort, and had made some pouches out of caribou hooves. They were not very easy to use, but I liked the one he gave me—it fit in with the rest of my not very typical life and its trappings.

The best thing to do with salmon, I learned, is to smoke it over aromatic wood until it has a flavor and tenderness that defies description. Bill immediately set up a smoking pit with an open-ended cover like a miniature Quonset hut. The salmon smoked for several hours and when we finally feasted, we must have sounded like we were in pain—we kept moaning, it was so good.

I couldn't figure out why Ken was with Lana, they were so unlike in character. My first impression of her as being a hippie was true. She wore a flowered skirt and Indian-print peasant blouse and appeared to be the embodiment of a "flower child." She moved deliberately, as though awed by her surroundings, or high, and had a kind of affected accent. She seemed out of place but entirely at ease with the mountains and the mountain men.

During their visit, I grew to like Lana's quirkiness, as well as how she treated me like a sister, taking care of me. As I cooked, she helped a bit, and it was good to have a female companion. She even sewed a patch on my jeans and said she put some "magic" in the pocket for me. Ken and Lana stayed almost a week, and it was a productive but tiring time. Bill and Ken shored up loose boards in the barn and secured the fencing around the corral. Lana helped me with canning and garden chores, and I delved into cleaning and cooking. I was pleasantly exhausted at the end of every day. I wrote to my parents that I felt like I was becoming quite the homemaker, juggling and keeping up with so many tasks.

There was some comfort in knowing that Bill had true friends; his long-term friendship with someone so kind and non-judgmental made me feel easier about his character. Ken felt that Bill was his "brother-from-another-mother"—their bond was that deep.

One afternoon not long after Ken and Lana had left, I heard a car drive up through the meadow road. I stepped outside the cabin door to see two ladies with bouffant hair-dos, dressed in skirts and high heels, get out of their large, blue, late-'60s sedan, briefcases in hand. Bill had already approached them and was standing with his arms crossed, chest puffed out, head back slightly. He was in charge, and not about to let strangers enter the property without his approval.

I sifted through the elements of this puzzling scene and came up with Jehovah's Witnesses. Of course. Who else would drive a logging road for sixty miles to find every last living soul that might be converted?

Bill was amusing himself by engaging them in some kind of battle of conviction, but they finally gave up and left when he told them his garden was growing so well this year thanks to the last Witnesses who'd ventured to Val Halla. He liked to jab at people's sensitivities—perhaps to see if he could make them uncomfortable, perhaps to enhance his image as an outsider. Probably both. It was an odd picture to see them next to Bill, dressed in his full buckskins and beaded headband, but they were the ones clearly out of place, standing there on the rutted dirt road covered with horse manure and goat droppings and both goats milling about to investigate. No doubt they'd heard of the renegade at the border and taken on the visit as a challenge.

After the women left, I asked Bill if there really had been other Witness visits. He told me they came up there, religiously, at least every couple of years. I couldn't decide who was more stubborn.

✗

CHAPTER TWENTY-TWO

*O*n Friday, August 23, Dad penned a letter to me about
President Ford and then responded to my negative
spin about privileged society, and especially the long abuses
of the white race over indigenous cultures.

Dearest Annie,

*The country now has a new president—fortunately for us all. He
may not be a great leader but I truly think he will be a good man
and will lift us away from our present tragedy. Our country,
contrary to what you may think, is not bad though of course we can
and should work to make it better. Land . . . land is what one makes
of it. The Arabs are making use of theirs by pumping oil from
beneath it. Do you think that is bad? I certainly do not. Do you
think by any wild stretch of the imagination no more building, no
more development should go on in our country? Impossible I would
say. The very things you think about would be impossible without
man's incredible drive to conquer nature . . . agreed some of it has
been poorly thought out but God, and I do believe in an almighty,
has not made any of his creatures perfect.*

*I would say humbly that you need to seriously study the
wonders of man and not criticize his flaws. Maybe from what I
glean Bill might benefit by so doing. I cannot believe that men who
live in cities are either base, stupid, but on the contrary, they are the*

 ones who have brought us to where we are. They have brought man to the kind of height which the human mind cherishes. Not just material things either. Medicine, art, literature, science have been brought to man by men of cities of great urban empires. Even the Aztecs were city people.

No, in my view it is not the lonely hunter, but the man of letters, of the challenge of urban life who left the best and brightest stamp on mankind. Getting back to land a minute. Bill apparently doesn't own any land but is tending it for someone else. The owners on the other hand have the real and legal responsibility for it. They must pay taxes & insurance at the very least. Let me point out something to you and Bill. You note I wrote insurance. It probably never crossed your mind nor his, that the owner of that land, were you hurt there could be sued for damages probably far exceeding the value of his land for any injuries sustained by you so land is not just a piece of ground . . . it carries all kinds of responsibilities and as valuable as it is today it should no longer be used for one's self alone. You are the one thinking about a starving world and you are saying we should rip out our roses. How many mouths are you feeding? What are you producing? Without scientific farming of which you know absolutely nothing you and the rest of man would have starved. No, my girl, you are very naive or blind.

But I love you and want you back.

Ever your Dad

I answered on August 26, while our thoughts were still fresh and engaged.

Dear Dad,

Maybe man has invented and created many miraculous and beautiful things—but WHITE MAN can also be accredited with destroying several cultures, including his own, whereas the Indian survived for 10s of thousands of years maintaining a balance with nature and among their own people—did they ever steal from the earth, strip her bare of what she had to offer? No—and always they gave to her—they were the children of nature, more knowledgeable in her ways than any other cultures, maybe what they gave to the earth doesn't show now, but at least it wasn't filth and grime that would be passed on—and were they men of letters? They were people of the sun and wind and soil—they were a culture with a universal language—sign language—they were men of soul and wisdom, not mechanical genius or "smartness."

So, maybe we have all benefited from what the modern world of medicines & rocket ships has produced, but also we have destroyed much of what was once beautiful and now we destroy ourselves. You see? I'm afraid I cannot look only at the good side of what White Man has done—for isn't he the one generally at fault for buying and selling nations & lives? For bombs and push-button warfare, for a faulty religion in which there is no belief in themselves, they only live for Money—to make the future brighter— the white American cannot live for today.

Whereas the far eastern Janists, Buddhists etc learn to love themselves, learn inner peace then work outward and strive for that peace in a universal way—seldom do you hear them speak loudly or harshly. Sure, I believe in a maker, but not the Christian way. Maybe I am blind about many things—but I've studied the origins of man, the history of man, the geography of man, and have studied especially the Indian cultures, and later how they were destroyed, not by themselves, but through the greed and blindness of the White man—maybe we are all blind as we have not touched the earth—for this I'm sorry and fear the destiny of man.

I love you, too, very much—

Dad's letters filled me. Even if I didn't agree with him, he was thoughtful and generous. Every act had a purpose; every question was a tool to find a better way to travel through the world. He held a positive view—believed in beauty and fulfillment and sought both. His heart was transparent and his thoughts clear as he expressed his fears and hopes for his children, and his ideals. I couldn't argue against his reminders that mankind had accomplished brilliant work, that a beautiful symphony penetrated the soul, that our ability to appreciate was a supreme gift. He countered my negative spin on the "White Man" to point out the goodness in mankind.

At times Dad's letters frustrated me, often made me smile, and always made me consider my part in the big picture. But at seventeen, I had to decide for myself what was valuable. Dad and I didn't often share the same sense of place in the world when it came to our personal contributions or priorities, but our love for each other was greater than our differences, and I understood that as something rare and special and true.

August was coming to a close, and the weather had been beautiful—cool nights and warm days and very little rain.

The river was getting low, but was very comfortable to wash and swim in. During my daily trips down to fill the five-gallon water jug, I noticed changes in the insect life near the river's edge, where the rocks were exposed close to the bank. There were shells of big, leggy bugs all over the rocks, but I didn't see the insect associated with them. Later, I would learn that they were larval husks of caddis flies, another river resident. People who came up to fish were not having much luck because of the water levels and flow, and Bill never took his rod out that summer.

It was time to make the serious push to prepare for winter. The cupboards were stocked with dried beans, rice, and other staples, but we still had to harvest the root vegetables, rebuild the root house, pick and can the last of the huckleberries, and cut the winter's wood.

The woodpile was diminishing and it was time to cut the winter's supply before the cold weather set in. Bill said we needed at least six cords to get through the cold from October to May. (A cord is a stack measuring four-by-four-by-eight—a total of 128 cubic feet.) The best source of wood around was the stand of dead tamarack snags about eight miles away that had been burned and cured in a forest fire. The tamarack, or larch, is a feathery and stately conifer, the only one that is deciduous. When the yellow-gold needles rain down in the fall, the forest floor is transformed into a golden carpet.

The morning that we headed out to cut some winter cordwood was chilly but clear, and the sun promised to warm the air. It would be a long day, so Bill told me to pack sandwiches for both of us, and to bring jackets and gloves. He tightened the blade on the chain saw, brought chain oil and an extra gallon of gas, and grabbed the two-man cross-cut saw and axes from the wood shed.

I rarely rode in the truck, and I was feeling anxious because our day would require all the strength and staying
power I could muster. I hoped to be able to manage the
work. While we were driving along, a song by Laura Nero—
"Wedding Bell Blues"—kept going through my head. It
wasn't a song I particularly liked, but it was about a man
named Bill and had been recently popular, and it seemed to
make its way into my brain when I was feeling a little closer
to Bill. Maybe I thought that cutting wood together was a
piece of the love puzzle.

We arrived at the stand of tamarack that was easiest to
get to and cut, and Bill chose the tree he wanted. First, he
explained how we would cut at an angle into the tree to
keep pressure off the saw blade, and what to do when the
tree began to fall. A tree trunk can spin and thrust up or
back as it goes down, and if you're in the path of the trunk,
that's not a good thing. Bill's warnings issued, we went to
work with the crosscut saw.

The tree was about two feet in diameter and at least
sixty feet high, and we started sawing a cut three feet off
the ground. I grew tired much sooner than I thought I
would and needed a rest. Bill showed me how to use my
whole body and not just my arms and I would have more
leverage for cutting. Then he joked around about the shape
of the handle and its motion, teasing with a little sexual
innuendo, suggesting that it could inspire me. I just rolled
my eyes.

We worked on the cut for the better part of half an hour,
then the tree creaked and Bill yelled for me to go a certain
direction to stay clear of the path of that big snag. As it
tipped and crashed down, the base of the trunk twisted and
threw itself into the air, and its falling was a surprising
event, shaking the ground under our feet and landing with a

booming noise that surrounded us. I had never been near a tree of that size coming down. As it settled, stillness and silence filled the space, then evaporated with our movement.

Once it was on the ground, I was charged with marking the tree every eighteen inches with a chalk so Bill could cut stove lengths. He poured gas and chain oil into the old chainsaw, yanked it to roaring, and the feel of day changed from a quiet and controlled effort to a hurried and desperate whining force. I understood the need for power to complete the job, but preferred my role that day as a sawyer with my one hundred pounds of energy.

Bill finished the cuts as I rolled the tree rounds closer to the truck. We tossed them in and stacked them, and I was drained. Time for lunch, and a rest.

As we sat, I watched Bill reach over to a rotted log, pick off a huge ant, longer than half an inch, and pop it into his mouth. "Just like a lemon drop," he said. He was enjoying the look of incredulity on my face. But it was only there for a wash of seconds. I didn't want him to think that I was so surprised or impressed. I could eat an ant too, no big deal.

He told me they had a body acid similar to citric acid (formic acid), and a little bit of crunch, but to be sure to pinch their pincers before they went in your mouth since they were carpenter ants and chewed through trees for their livelihood. I grabbed one by the head between my index finger and thumb and put it in my mouth. Then I ate another to prove my lack of squeamishness and confirm the flavor. It was true—they tasted tart like lemon, and I imagined baking them into cookies. I wasn't about to make insects a regular part of my diet, but here Bill was yet again, changing my concepts about resources in the wild and daring me to step outside of my boundaries.

✗

CHAPTER TWENTY-THREE

*W*hen I went out to our mailbox on Tuesday, August 27, there was a letter from Mom, written the previous Saturday. Her note opened with the sad news that my dad's sister—his only sibling, Joan—had died of an apparent heart attack and drowned in their pool in Spain. Joan was only forty-eight and had been a strong swimmer, even though compromised by polio. My parents were stunned and grieving, and my grandmother, Didi, had fallen apart. My mom informed me she'd had to be sedated.

Family had rallied around, and my sister and oldest brother were there with Mom to help with my grandmother and offer Dad support. Mom wrote he was feeling lonely and lost, and I ached for him. He would travel to be with family in Connecticut, and attend her service and burial once they returned from Spain. I thought about my aunt's invitation when we'd visited them after my graduation, urging me to join them that summer in Spain instead of carrying through with my Montana plan, and I felt uneasy imagining the trauma for my family and how I might have been there if I was not in Montana.

The news about my aunt was heartbreaking. Joan had emanated strength—something she'd had to muster to raise a family with almost no use of her arms. She'd also been witty, and beautiful, and I'd thought of her as special in my family circle. I sent a letter right away on August 28 to let my parents know how sad and sorry I was for Dad and Didi and my Connecticut family. I'd had some dreams, prior to receiving Mom's letter, that seemed foretelling, so I described them for my parents.

Dear Mom & Dad,

I had strange dreams warning me of what was going to happen. About a month or so ago I dreamed first that Bill had drowned in the river—right after that, the same night a dream about someone of [Joan's family/children] drowning came into focus. Seriously I was going to write Jock [Joan's son] the next day and tell him, knowing he was [home in Connecticut] this summer—and just in the past few days I've thought many times about my cousins and the times I've spent with them. So maybe there were premonitions of her death—such an incredibly strong and soulful person—owning a patience and beauty that few can claim, a will and power ran fierce in her blood. So much to give. Joanie [was] a true, good person in every way.

Another dream I remember, from last week. I was riding and saw the Thunderbird [Mom's car] arrive at the nearby cabin, when I went in, Mom, you and Jen had been crying, and we all just stood there, not knowing what to say, but that is where the dream ended. If there's any connection I don't know, but I'm well aware of the powers of the inner or sixth sense, and must take heed when it is trying to communicate something.

I love you both so very much, take good care, take sweet silence and love,

Annie

Mom wrote back on the fifth of September to thank me for my thoughts about my aunt, and let me know that Dad was in Connecticut with family while she stayed home to help look after Didi, who could not travel to her daughter's funeral. She also said that now that she was "quite sure" that I would be wintering at Val Halla, she would be sending some supplies and clothes soon.

The first days of September were crisp, and we woke to frost two days in a row. The fresh garden greens wilted, and Bill told me the root crops would sweeten in the ground with the cold temperatures. There were still a few huckleberries and currants ready to pick and process, so we spent part of an afternoon gleaning the last of them nearby.

There was an ongoing conversation in my mind to firm up that I would be staying with Bill, and I was going through the motions of physically preparing for winter. I was not willing to entertain the possibility of leaving. When I next wrote to Mom and Dad on September 3, I tried to clarify previous thoughts that had conveyed feelings of frustration, or even despair. I wanted to convince them that I was not unhappy or lonely and intended to stay in Montana; anything short of that would be a failure. I explained that it would be impossible to live under their roof, at the same time trying to soften my rebuttal of their ideals and lifestyle with the simple fact that I would not want to infringe on their world. The notion of going to college "turned me off," and the only way I could manage leaving would be to find a similar life somewhere remote. I was starting to understand the scope of the work required to maintain a home off the grid, take care of animals, even nurture a relationship. But I was still very new at it and had lots to learn before I could take care of myself. Bill was not a brute, I assured them. I respected him and I would do my best to learn and help him as long as I was living at Val Halla. Maybe I would be home the next summer to visit, I suggested, and closed with a request for them to be patient and not worry about me.

CHAPTER TWENTY-FOUR

*B*read was rising and Bill was busy preparing part of a hide to put in the smokehouse so he could make some gloves as I wrote to my parents on September 10. The days were chilly and nights frosty now and we were expecting the first snow any time, but the first few days of September had been warm enough for a river trip down the North Fork with three college students who were staying at one of the fishing cabins. They had brought a canoe and rubber raft and invited us to join them for a paddling adventure downriver to Polebridge, where they had left a truck the previous day. I wanted to write home right away to describe our twenty-three-mile raft and canoe trip.

It felt a little out of character for Bill to want to join the boys for a raft trip to Polebridge, since it meant a whole day away from chores and projects around the cabin. But it also presented a physical challenge and a ride down a beautiful section of the North Fork of the Flathead, both of which appealed to him. I, meanwhile, was excited to adventure with the others; it would be a reprieve from my routine and a chance to be engaged in a way I enjoyed.

There was room in the raft for three, so I rode with Tom and his friend Mike while Bill and Guy paddled the canoe. The first six miles was slow-going since the water level was low, and there were lots of pebbly riffles that we had to nudge the low-riding raft over or even get out and walk the raft through. It was cumbersome, and I told my parents it was like navigating a "pregnant donut." The canoe had an easier time of it; it rode low in the water and had to be walked over several shallow spots, but it was beautifully graceful through the rapids.

One incident caught everyone by surprise. Bill and Guy were ahead of the three of us, and as we approached a chute with a short but steep rapids, we saw Bill step out of the canoe to lift a log that blocked the chute so Guy could paddle beneath it. Instead of ducking, however, Guy grabbed on to the log, pulling himself out and dumping the canoe. We watched the episode from our raft as if it were in slow motion, then dropped through the chute, hurrying to reach Bill and Guy in case they needed help—but we soon saw them paddling downstream with all of our gear, wet but aboard.

Soon after, we stopped for lunch to dry and rest. We had a spectacular view of the high rugged peaks to the east. The river was pristine, the water turquoise-colored either from the glacial runoff or the limestone in the rock ledges, and so clear that even over a deep hole in a quiet bend the bottom was crystalline. Where the sun pierced the surface, the slab rock under the water appeared lit from inside and glowed a brilliant emerald green, and I described it to my parents as "beauty unimaginable." We drank from it every day and never got sick, so it wasn't surprising to see the bottom of the river even eight feet down.

About halfway to Polebridge, a miniature whirlwind created a funnel of water that touched down on the river, lifting a shaft of mist that spun up to what seemed like a hundred feet—an unusual event that left us all staring at the sky.

Nine or ten hours after we started the trip, we reached

the Polebridge store/outpost, hungry and muscles aching. As we carried our boats across the parking lot we joked about the canoe accident, and what if the truck keys were on the bottom of the river? Then Guy pulled them from his pocket with a big grin. We loaded the boats and our gear and Bill and I rode home in the back of the truck with Tom.

I was exhausted and quiet as we drove through the early evening; Bill was lively and invigorated. This was the kind of challenge he loved because it showed his strength and know-how, and gave him material for his stories. He was social, in spite of setting himself apart from people, and that day he seemed relaxed and genuinely happy, as if he had settled into just being with others and not feeling like he had to perform in a role.

Our day on the river filled me with something I had been missing. The shared effort, challenge, and laughter acted like a tonic and I felt refreshed and easy. But it was a singular event, and the feelings were ephemeral.

A couple of days after our raft trip, on September 11, Guy came by the cabin in the morning to let us know that they were heading to Polebridge for some supplies and ask if we needed anything or wanted to join them. Bill wasn't interested in going but said I was free to do as I pleased, so I got some cash from my wallet and jumped into the truck with Guy and Tom, eager for an excursion with new friends, and to pick up a couple of grocery items. I also had it in mind to call home.

The phone was an old-fashioned box with the two bells and a mouthpiece, hung on a post right in the middle of the store. I had to go through an operator to call collect. My brother Geof answered, and was quite surprised to hear my voice. Mom was home, and she picked up the phone in another room so I could talk to both of them at once. I wanted to be close, say important things, tell them stories about my world, and have every word count, but the conversation felt incomplete. At least they knew I was fine. Mom sounded concerned and maybe even a little upset; she may have been feeling the same frustration of not being able to express things fully. I felt I had to edit myself because the folks who ran the store were tuned in my direction. They were, after all, more than curious about Bill and his doings.

Before we left the Polebridge store we shopped for a few provisions. For a treat I bought bananas and oranges, since it had been months since I had eaten either one. The bananas were on their way to overripe, so I aspired to baking some kind of birthday cake with them; even though I had no intention of announcing my birthday the next day, it would be special for me. I didn't want to tell Bill it was my birthday and raise expectations, although I'd dropped a hint or two.

✕

CHAPTER TWENTY-FIVE

*M*om wrote Saturday, September 7, to wish me a
happy birthday, and it arrived on mail day, Tuesday, September 10.

Dearest Annie

*Happy happy 18th! You now have your own, very own, wings and
are free to live in Montana or wherever without having to have
parental permission. Seriously, though, I'm sure you realize the
responsibilities and boundaries that accompany your freedom; but
know that you will always have our love—and guidance & support
whenever you want or need it.*

Two days later, I wrote this journal entry:

September 12 1974

*So, on this twelfth September day, which also happens to be my 18th
birthday, we woke to a sun which lit the snow dusted peaks to a
brilliance that only the sun can create. It has been a long while that
I have written down any thoughts, and much has been learned and
seen in between.*

*Now, though Bill reminds me that I've not done as I ought to
have, we are closer and feelings are warmer . . .*

My birthday had always marked the beginning of a new school year, and with it a sense of moving forward. But my birthday in Montana was a time to think about endings; childhood was officially behind me, summer was gone, and fall was moving in with winter not far behind. It brought a sense of quiet and isolation. I imagined what it would be like to winter so far from people, in a snowbound cabin with a man I did not feel at home with.

That morning was cold, but we got an early start for a day of work on the root house. Bill planned to use Jeremiah to help haul bridge timbers that had washed out from the border bridge in a flood a year or two earlier. The timbers were ideal for rebuilding the root house, which was tiny and caving in. Four solid ten-by-ten posts would support the roof rafters, and the massive two-by-ten planks would provide a sturdy roof. The design was simple, almost like a kiva but square, with the four posts to hold the heavy cross-timbers and roofing planks that would be covered by dirt for insulation.

Bill had spent the better part of two days removing dirt from the sides and floor of the old root house to make a larger space. It took the entire morning to haul the timbers the fifty yards from where they had lodged downstream of the cabin. We dragged them up the bank, then secured rope around the ends one at a time so we could lash it to the hitch behind Jeremiah, who seemed eager to be employed. Bill sat astride him while they worked together to pull the timbers to the staging area behind the cabin. The clear, crisp morning slowly warmed, the river sparkled, and the anticipation and excitement around building something new made the work go quickly.

As Bill worked to prepare the timbers and clear the area for construction, I went inside to bake my spiced banana and orange cake. While it was in the oven, I cut up rutabaga, carrots, parsnips, onions, beet greens, peppers, green beans, and cabbage into a big pot, added generous pieces of moose and elk meat from the canned provisions, and let it simmer to a rich stew for our supper later. The cabin smelled of oranges and cloves and the pungent rutabaga, and I was excited about our special dinner. Guy, Tom, and Mike stopped by briefly to say goodbye and give us the rest of their groceries, including milk, which tasted heavy but not as flavorful as goat milk; I was sad to see them go.

After lunch Bill had some time to give me a lesson about the scraping process in tanning hides. He had a deer hide that he'd soaked in a smelly mashed brain and water bath to soften the tough fibers so they could be scraped clean of hair and softened before the hide was ready to cure in the smoke house. The hide was now drying on a rack but was not completely dry, so it was the ideal time to scrape.

Scrapers are about eight inches long, slightly curved, and blunt-bladed. To scrape with them, you have to continually pull down with small chopping motions in order to remove the hair and start to break down the fibrous hide. It surprised me to find out how rigorous it was; every few minutes I needed a rest, and by the end of that first session only managed to scrape a part of the hide. Bill reminded me that Helen had become very good at it during their time together; "as strong as squaw," he said, noting that Indian women could scrape several hides in a day. The point he was making, not lost on me, was that Helen was more capable with the necessary skills and chores than I was. Any time Bill made a comparison to Native Americans it was in a positive light—having to do with their strength or their good methods for living on the land.

In the afternoon, around five o'clock, we headed out on

foot to scout for bear sign and small game like grouse. Bill mentioned that he would like to kill a bear before winter for the hide and meat and, more importantly, the grease. I assumed he meant black bear; he'd mentioned scouting for grizzly but I was sure that he wouldn't kill one, because he had the highest respect for them. I figured he just wanted to get a glimpse of the great bear. He occasionally reminded me how lucky I was to have had such a peaceful encounter with a griz and her cub, and I suspected he wanted his own experience.

Bill's ability to spot animal tracks, scat, and other animal signs was finely tuned, and I was impressed by his keen sense of surroundings. We had seen three white-tailed deer at the edge of the meadow the day before, so we knew that animals were getting ready for cold weather and either moving to their wintering grounds or preparing for hibernation. As I followed in Bill's path, carrying a rifle, I tried to walk silently and not to snap twigs and rustle leaves, but I was hoping we wouldn't spot any animals. I knew hunting was a critical skill for wilderness survival but I really didn't want to shoot anything, that day or ever.

We wandered back empty-handed and ready for dinner. The stew was creamy and rich after I thickened it with a roux of a little flour and bear grease and some milk, and it was one of the best meals we had enjoyed. Bill especially liked the banana orange spice cake. He asked me if this was a special occasion—like a birthday, maybe? I flashed a smile and told him yes, happy to have a little celebration inserted quietly at the end of a productive, positive day.

At dusk the temperature dropped to 25 degrees, but the cabin was warm and I decided to give myself a nice sponge bath near the stove. Around nine o'clock Bill jumped up from the couch where he was reading when he remembered that he had intended to harvest the beets. He told me to suit up and get a flashlight while he grabbed a shovel and bucket. With my hair still wet, out we went to dig and collect the beets in the darkness.

When I wrote to Mom and Dad the next morning to describe my very busy birthday, I mentioned that my call home was awkward because there was almost too much to say so I'd been at a loss for words. I said I was sorry that Dad and I had missed each other, and sent extra hugs. Then I went through my upcoming day, which included doing a tub of laundry in the river, cleaning the cabin, and maybe getting a little further into my book. I was reading *Papillon*, by Henri Charrière, and was already totally engrossed by the intense autobiographical account of his prison escape in the 1930s from a penal colony.

Once again I confirmed that I was happily settling into Val Halla, even as I expressed unveiled concern about winter: "Yes, I love this life, and it isn't as worthless as you might think, for surely I've not been defeated yet, and I'm becoming stronger physically and mentally—but the real trial will be to see how well I winter here—the cold silence, the winds, the isolation. Right now there are still people milling around the valley, and so all is not deserted, and even in winter the valley is accessible via snowmobile (curse their noisy motors) —but winter, Bill says, is the time for thinking and doing all the things that were wanting to be done in the summer, only lacking time. (I have all my own time, though chores take up much of it, but even so I enjoy the physical work very much. Strange, because I never even emptied the trash at home, or cooked anything more than a hot dog)."

Dad sent his own, belated letter to wish me a happy eighteenth birthday (it arrived a day or two after the twelfth).

Annie Dearest,

Imagine today you're 5840 days old. Some number. I have liked counting those days. All good if you ask me. It's cold here and it must be more so there. We've had a trace of snow and the leaves have started to shed summer's green. I love fall but spring is best of all. Eighteen springs for you that's the best way of looking at it.

Geof leaves today which cuts us down to Josie, so it's a mixed bag of a day. Golly I was sorry not to hear your cheery voice the other day. Maybe you'll call again soon. Telephones are good once in a while.

God bless
Love, Dad

CHAPTER TWENTY-SIX

*D*uring the next few days, Bill started the work on the root house, and I pitched in here and there when he needed help. We cross-cut the timbers to length, some that measured an impressive twenty inches in width, and got ready to build. We were already harvesting beets, rutabagas and carrots, so the root house was fast becoming a priority. Bill needed the space to store canned foods there, as well as eggs, which can be preserved for quite some time if one end is dipped in vinegar and the other in wax, and then stored wax-side-up in sand. A root house maintains a constant temperature of about 55 degrees because it is below ground, and the roots and canned food would keep through the winter.

Bill was a good designer and an exacting builder. "Measure twice, cut once," he advised as he laid out the boards and marked them for rafters and cross beams. It was the first time I'd heard that tidbit of wisdom, and it was the perfect mantra for the job. He emphasized that a person's work is "only as good as his tools." That is especially true when your survival depends on certain tools, and hand tools at that. Besides the cross-cut saw, we used a couple of hammers, a ruler, a pencil, a tomahawk, and sharpened chisels for cleaning up the notches where the timbers would join. We also used a shovel, small hand drills, a screwdriver and screws for the hinges, and some enormous old eight-inch-long burnt nails that Bill straightened with his hammer.

To get down into the cellar, we would need steps, so Bill cut two stringers and four treads from the heavy timbers that he notched into place for a very solid fit. Then we dug holes for four heavy ten-inch diameter timbers for the posts near the corners of the space. Bill cut rafters that he fit to span the posts, and once they were nailed in place we laid wide planks on them for the ceiling. It was high enough that I could stand up with room to spare, and Bill just brushed those ceiling planks. It was beautiful and a generous space, measuring ten by twelve feet. We cut the remaining planks to build shelves and the three-by-three-foot bins along both walls on the floor that would hold the stores of vegetables, and Bill built a bulkhead-type door.

Later that week we put a plastic sheet on top of the rafters and shoveled dirt over it for insulation, so outside the roof was about a foot higher than the ground level. Then the root house was tight and ready for winter.

My journal entry September 14 read like a pep talk, trying to convince myself that with more time and effort, some of the basic skills and pleasures that I expected from the homesteading way of life would fall into place.

Waking now to cooler, darker mornings, soon we'll be up at 7:00 seeming like we're up in the middle of the night. Sept. 14 now, and winter weather is drawing near—Bill has been working hard on the root cellar, and I helped carry the bridge timbers yesterday, so that it has a roof now. Still Wayne has not brought up the chain saw, so today we'll take the cross cut and go for snags.

Bill told me yesterday that Joe & Flo mentioned that they felt I wasn't going to stay while he was gone on his trip. That irks me. No trust, or belief in people and their word. Though I know full well that many people's word . . . cannot be trusted. Lately Bill has had love (and Helen) on the brain—maybe it's leading up to his feelings for me—still I don't love him, perhaps in a slight way, sort of like a brother, but if it were love, I'd know, and that funny feeling in the stomach hasn't hit yet. At least that's what I've heard you feel when in love.

. . . Mom and Dad will be off for Europe soon, hope it is relaxing and the time goes smoothly for them, because my love for them is strong—and the bonds will never break.

Am getting into Papillon, my god what a horrendous, strong book! His will makes me feel weak.

Woink just keeps eating & growing & growing & eating—-my, my—he'll be good bacon come fall! But I think Bill and I certainly will miss him. Unfortunately, he has become quite a character & companion. The only pig I've ever heard of riding—just hop on him, kick his sides a couple of times and we're off in flash of light!

Worked on part of a hide the other day—those Indian women must have been super-strong to do several hides a day—never a complaint, and always working on a beautiful piece of beadwork, or something like that. Yes, I have all this time, but it is not the same time as even an Indian squaw had—sure she had kids to care for, food to cook, hides & heavy work to do, but no laundry, no floors to mop, dishes to do—still I strive for that kind of strength . . . and the spirit . . . Hope to be able to shoot & throw a tomahawk, but like everyone knows, it takes practice and so I'd better get moving and start to get at it.

By this time, I did have the know-how and confidence to do much of the work on my own. I was enjoying an evening alone as I wrote a letter to Dad by the light of our kerosene lamp. The canning kettle was whistling with the last batch of green beans, and I mentioned to Dad that I was cooking the little banty hen. I'd found her dead that morning and butchered her for the stew pot.

It was Tuesday, September 17, and we had just received a letter that day from Bill's parents to let us know that they were planning to drive from Florida to visit and would be arriving in the next few days, so Bill decided to drive the truck down to Kalispell for some supplies, and told me he'd be back the next day.

Writing to Dad, I mused that fall was my favorite time, thinking about the Aspen trees turning gold in the Colorado mountains and the "kaleidoscope of reds, browns, oranges, golds, yellows, and the smell of crispy air and pumpkin and fallen leaves" in the East, "like the calm before a storm, knowing winter will soon be here." Leaves were just starting to turn from yellow to brown, but with no more color than that. Bill had told me that the river would turn to gold when the leaves made their way to the water to be carried downstream, and I wanted to share that image with Dad, describing the light at dawn when the water sparkled and flowed with golden leaves.

I was feeling homesick, and it helped to wrap myself in a conversation with Dad. In spite of the melancholy, I was determined to sound positive, and I veered into a gushing proclamation of our mutual love. And I addressed Dad's sweet note about how many days I'd been on this earth, saying in closing, "Those 5,840 days went by all too quickly, and I must say I'm rather sad to see childhood go away just like that (though I still keep and cherish my childlike ways) but am looking forward to many many more days . . . & know that I love you more than life itself."

The next day was warm and clear when Bill arrived back from Kalispell in the early afternoon with an armload of supplies including extra toilet paper, black tea, coffee for his dad, and a bushel of apples. After supper we went out into the evening and were surprised and lucky to see an Aurora Borealis event. It looked like a ribbon of luminous green ink that had been spread across the surface of the sky above us with a giant dropper, and we were below to see it cascading down through the darkness. It was truly wondrous.

Joe and Flo had been up for a few days, and when I walked across the meadow to visit the next day, they asked if we had seen the Aurora Borealis, so we shared our experience. I was growing fond of them, and was a little disappointed that they had mentioned to Bill that they thought I might not stay at Val Halla, but I didn't bring it up, thinking they would see that I was determined and sturdy enough once winter arrived. A few weeks had passed since Bill's pack trip, and I wanted to think that they now understood I was tougher than they'd assumed. Bill had almost said as much when he let me know about that conversation with them.

CHAPTER TWENTY-SEVEN

*M*om had sent a couple of postcards to let me know that she was busy with home life and working on painting a portrait for a friend. It made me happy to think of her painting because she was so talented, and it gave her something to do other than housework or taking care of aging parents. She had also sent a box filled with wool socks, soap, stamps, and the book *Touch the Earth*, by T.C. McLuhan, which I'd asked her to send so that Bill could read it.

Bill read *Touch the Earth* right away and absorbed the message as I had, moved by the prayer-like depiction of the land and its original inhabitants, living in harmony with nature, and the ensuing destruction of that harmony when the White Man arrived. Since we shared an interest in Native American culture, we discussed some of the history we had read. I told him about *The Long Death*, by Ralph Andrist, a clear and distressing account about the dispossession of the Plains Indians after 1840, and said I would ask Mom to send it for him to read. There was no justification for the wanton destruction of whole cultures, and we agreed about that. It was one of the few topics that we were able to talk about as equals, since he respected my interest and passion about Native American culture and history. We both wanted to model our life after those aspects of a culture we didn't belong to but revered.

I wrote to Mom to thank her for the box and told her about our new root house and our late-summer warm weather, but even before my letter landed at home Mom sent her own letter to tell me about her painting and included her response to my previous hostile sentiments about the White Man and our broken modern culture.

Friday, September 20

Dearest Annie,

It's been great of you to write so often, so descriptively & so well. I thoroughly understand your passion for what you're doing because I've had more than a taste of it. What I don't understand is your total denigration of "White Man" & your complete sympathy with the American (early) Indian. They didn't choose their way of life— they were faced with it & learned to cope. If they had had some of our modern conveniences no doubt they would have used them. The old adage "necessity is the mother of invention" is why we have electric drills, washing machines, automotive transportation, plumbing and all the other creature comforts, including the vast knowledge & accessibility to medicine & science. I'm not saying that today's world is rosy; some aspects and some people are destructive, but there are many fine and creative humans in this world and there always have been. Unfortunately our news media reports mostly the worst, & we become biased & disillusioned. But great things are happening constantly & I hope that someday you will be in touch with them: I hope also that the commencement message from Agnes De Mille is not forgotten.

The American Indian was inhabiting Mesa Verde at the time Christ was born & the beginning of the ten commandments which to me are a great and important guideline. I don't necessarily think they are timeless, but if all peoples were to follow them this would be a utopian, (if not somewhat sterile) world. The Indians had their own guidelines, based on necessity, superstition and intuition. They were primitive at a time when certain civilizations were at, or past, their prime. They were still primitive when the great Renaissance was at its peak.

Annie love, I can't continue to philosophize right now as I must get to market & take Manna to the doctor. However I must point out 2 things: one—if all people lived the way you and Bill are there would be no wilderness left—two—you are a built-in servant & convenience for Bill, regardless of the fact that you are learning, appreciating & enjoying.

How can you bear to kill & eat Woink & wear the kitten's mittens??

Much much love,

Mom (the weather is cold & windy.)

No matter how much I loved my parents, I didn't believe that their luxury was a God-given right, or that their appreciation of beauty should allow them to ignore a recent past that was filled with the aggression of settlers and soldiers displacing and killing Native Americans for the sake of expansion and ownership of resources. I knew that I was simplifying and categorizing history to suit my convictions, but that dark stain in our past could not be justified, period. I understood Mom to be saying that she had an admiration for the advances of civilization even though it had overrun the "primitive" cultures in this country, and that went against everything I felt and was why I had chosen to live apart from their world.

I wasn't sure what any of us could do about the trajectory toward what I feared would be a slow, sad destruction of our planet. But it was important to try to push my sense of what was so wrong with our privileged white society, because I wanted my parents to understand this critical piece of our history and why I felt urgent about the past, present, and future. They didn't like doom and gloom, and I felt like the messenger of darkness, but Mom's Pollyana attitude pushed me to be more adamant.

In answer to my mom I dared to enter into an argument with her, starting with, "I suppose you didn't read *Touch the Earth*, or else you wouldn't be so stubborn about where the Indian stood. Sure, he was put on this planet in a situation like everyone else was, but he could have invented dishwashers if he'd wanted to—or automobiles (well, he was wiped out before that era, or should I say because of that era)—but he honored his Mother, the Earth, respected her and did not rape her of her bounty as white man has."

Much of my letter to Mom was the same message I had recently sent to Dad, and to both of them at various other times. My views were firm, and unlikely to change. The respect for nature shown by native populations around the world made so much more sense to me than the worldview of the white man—that of dominating the planet, of extracting oil from the earth for cars or strip-mining mountains for coal.

I couldn't ignore the environmental destruction around the globe, which I attributed to Bill's premise that human activity was fueled and fouled by greed, hatred, and illusion. It didn't make me happy to think the way I did, but I responded to Mom that "the end result is a very sad one I'm afraid—certainly at the rate population is increasing, at the rate our natural resources are being used up, at the speed of technological devises being turned out to use & abuse energy, we will not be living here for very much longer—and if you doubt my word—just wait and see, because no one is doing anything about it—they hold the same attitude as you, 'if we die it serves us'—well you could be just joking—but honestly, it is bound that we're doomed."

As if I hadn't already shared a large enough dose of despair, I ended with a note about Woink's days being numbered. We would have to butcher him in a week or two. I hated to see him go. "But," I wrote, "the bacon & grease are necessary to keep us alive & well this winter—and I'm not too fond of the kittens—besides, I'll learn tanning & sewing of leathers." I did enjoy the kittens, but I tried every way I could to convince myself and others that making them into mittens was part of the life that I'd signed up for with Bill, since he had set up that challenge for me the day I arrived, and I couldn't get too sensitive about it.

Bill understood that I wanted to embrace his lifestyle for many of the same reasons that he did. Living as close to nature as possible and not participating in a culture of acquisition, waste, and destruction seemed like the only way I could mitigate the negative feelings I harbored about my privilege, my white expansionist heritage, and my own tendencies to enjoy the spoils of that culture. He had similar motivations, but his experience growing up in Florida, his time in Vietnam, and being a man shaped and colored his world view in a way I could never understand. The anger and disdain—or maybe it was fear—he harbored were not emotions he could address internally, and it made me uncomfortable to hear him condemn others who did not live or believe as he did, even though I was experiencing that same struggle with my parents in our letters back and forth. On occasion he would say something that smacked of racism in his thinly disguised references to people of color or Middle Eastern cultures, and that did not fit who I thought he should be; it was inconsistent with his reverence for Native American culture and in conflict with what I believed to be basic human decency. It seemed that Bill converted his emotions into a place of feeling superior, but I didn't believe that was a way to fix any predicament, personally or socially. Living in a society that he despised would have been intolerable for him, and his way of coping was to tap his determination and abilities to survive the homesteading life of a mountain man.

My frustration and disdain often manifested itself as sorrow, and was more generally directed at a culture gone wrong. If I thought that I could contribute in some way to reverse the negative trends that led to destruction of the environment or social injustice, I might have looked for a path instead of an escape hatch, but the long history of those abuses seemed too big and embedded in our society to fix. I admired those who did engage in trying to mitigate the environmental damage, create a just society, and live honorably, and there were plenty of role models. I was in awe of people I read about who seemed fearless in ways I couldn't fathom—like Jane Goodall, who dedicated her life to studying and saving great apes and their habitat, or Martin Luther King, Jr., who gave himself to the cause of trying to build a just and equitable society, or Jacques Cousteau, who showed us the immense and magnificent undersea world in a desperate attempt to save the oceans. These people were stars and I looked up to them, but I also admired people across the spectrum who were not famous but seemed brave or simply hard-working, like reporters in war zones, field hands, or those willing to lend aid in desperate situations.

I knew that there wasn't a perfect world, anywhere—no Heaven, Shangri-La, or Valhalla. But I had hoped that my own path would lead to a negotiable, peaceful, and rewarding life. Even though it was a way to avoid and negate the larger world, it seemed like the right recipe: move to a remote and beautiful place, learn to live off the land, pursue some creative activities, and share that home with someone caring.

But Bill was not that person, and life with him was growing uncomfortable. My dream of a loving relationship was just that. He was showing increasingly less patience for my mistakes and I felt on edge, struggling to feel deep commitment to him and his Val Halla. What was transpiring between us didn't show up as blame in any direction; rather, it evolved as a lack of joy or interest in one another.

When I tried to imagine what I could do if I left Montana, the vision was hazy. Maybe I could use my drawing skills to illustrate natural science or antiquities. Or I could work on a farm and learn more about food production. No matter what, if I left, I would have to find a way to create a life where I could feel productive, competent, and peaceful—and I would have to face the mess that was my life at home, including my own use of alcohol and pot, since it would be available and tempting again, and also the situation with my brother-in-law. The fix for that was elusive, and my current isolation was the only solution I'd come up with so far.

All of these feelings were held together in a loose matrix that I could only share obliquely with my parents, and they had no way to help me sort any of it out, except to offer their love and acceptance.

CHAPTER TWENTY-EIGHT

*B*ill's parents would be arriving any time, so I cleaned and readied my bedroom for them and did some extra housekeeping chores to make the cabin comfortable and welcoming. They would have to cope with no running water, using the outhouse, limited lighting, and our diet, so our cabin needed to be at least clean and orderly. I couldn't picture his mom and dad, even when he described them to me, because they sounded so unlike him. He called his mom "The Little Mother," but in an endearing way. He said his father was a "simple man." I was glad they were willing to stay connected, despite Bill's efforts to sever ties with so much of his past. Bill mentioned that he had written to them about me, but I didn't know what he had told them.

They would be spending a week with us, and I was excited to see their blue station wagon pull up in front of the cabin. My first impression of them proved to be true: they were kind and genuine, but neither one was easygoing.

Catherine seemed fragile and had serious, frequent headaches all week. There was seemingly nothing I could do to alleviate her pain, even though I warmed washcloths for her forehead and tried to make the cabin comfortable for her. As she rested on the couch off and on that week, we talked easily about things. She asked about my family and home in Colorado, and was interested in my relationship with my parents. When she asked me how I was getting along with Bill, I was surprised at how direct she was in her inquiries.

I gave her the edited version, trying to keep it in the positive arena. She made it clear that she knew her son could be hard to live with. I learned more about her upbringing, and that she'd attended college. Although she was very sensitive and controlled, she had a sense of humor, and it took the edge off her otherwise sharply drawn boundaries.

She worried so hard about things, including how to enjoy her son and his life, and the conflict must have caused her some discomfort. But at the dinner table, she engaged us with her opinions about the political climate, books she recommended, and her love of the arts. She was bright and well-read, and she held her ground with Bill; it seemed like she and Bill enjoyed sparring about politics and social issues.

There were definitely some differences of opinion that week. Catherine embraced her religious beliefs and softly insisted we should, too. I had nothing to add on that topic and mostly stayed in the background when she brought it up, feeling that it was not my place to enter the conversation. She also alluded to the trauma and sorrow of dealing with one of her other two sons, who was institutionalized in a psychiatric hospital, and I began to understand the depth of her grief.

Bill and his father, Andrew, were temperamentally polar opposites. Andrew was not feisty or opinionated; during our dinnertime discussions, he was quiet and seemed uncomfortable in the contest of discourse about intangibles like politics or history. He was much more at ease with the immediate needs of survival and maintenance. Having grown up in a large family of sharecroppers in the South, in a small shack without electricity, he understood hardship and hard work and was fit and strong. He kept himself busy helping with the chores and projects that week, working with Bill to finish the last details of the root house and make some repairs to the cabin chinking. He was eager to show us that he knew how to swing a hammer. He also busied himself in the garden, harvesting root vegetables with Bill and tucking them away in the new root house; it was nice to see the two of them working together and relaxed. When he offered to cook, I was pleasantly surprised, and he took over to prepare a few of our dinners, even washing the dishes—help I truly appreciated.

During a slow-moving and brilliant afternoon, I decided to take a ride with Jude. When I was halfway across the meadow, I turned around to see Bill following after us on Ahkee. He raced to catch up, then passed me. I nudged Jude into a run as we flew toward the beaver ponds at the far end of the meadow. There was no hurry to get back to the cabin, so Bill led us across the river and up onto a ridge toward the distant blue of the glacial peaks, and I drank in the view of the jagged range framed by the gold of the turning trees. We trailed the ridge then headed downhill to cross the North Fork just in front of the cabin. Catherine had been enjoying the sun and sitting on the bench on top of the river bank, watching for us to come back, and she took a snapshot of us just as we crossed below her.

Coming across the river from a ride
Photo credit: Catherine Atkinson

While his parents were still visiting, Bill suggested that we drive over to the Blackfoot Indian reservation in Browning, Montana, on the other side of Glacier Park, where he had planned to go on his pack trip before Ahkee escaped and forced him to cut the trip short. He wanted to visit with a sculptor friend and gallery owner there, and finally deliver the engraving of a bobcat that he'd created for him. Bill offered to drive his parents' station wagon, pitching the day as an adventure through Glacier Park and an interesting outing for all of us.

The trip one way was three hours driving down the logging road to Polebridge and the West Gate of Glacier Park, up and over Logan Pass on the Going-to-the-Sun Highway, and then out through the eastern side of the park. I was eager to see Glacier Park and glad for a trip to a town, the first since I'd arrived, but the hours sitting in the backseat of the car with Catherine were a strain; she seemed uncomfortable and exhausted instead of awed by the scenery, and I could not change that dynamic for her.

Bill was fully dressed in his buckskins and fur, even though it wasn't cold. He was a bit of a showman, probably a little more so that day because we were going onto an Indian reservation.

On Logan Pass in Glacier Park

Bill and his parents at the top of Logan Pass

Browning, which sat out on the plains east of the divide, was dry and barren. It made me uncomfortable to feel like a tourist in what was clearly not a tourist destination. Bill's outfit did get some attention, but the sideward glances in his direction from the few people on the street in the reservation town seemed wary. The whole day felt out of balance; Bill's friend was away, which greatly disappointed Bill, and we stayed in Browning just long enough to buy a fifty-pound bag of onions before beginning the three-hour trip home.

A day or two later, as Bill's parents packed the car to leave for home, they said goodbye to Woink before they hugged us and got in the car. They told Bill to be good to me; his mother had sensed our tenuous relationship and seemed to not want to see either of us hurt. Their visit had proven to be a bit of a trial, but we all understood the limits of our situation and had enjoyed the time together.

I was looking forward to getting back to our quiet routine, though a little sad to say goodbye. It had been nice to have a woman around, especially one who quietly supported me.

On Thursday, September 27, when I wrote home to tell Mom and Dad about the visit with Bill's parents, I watched out the window as enormous, wet snowflakes covered the ground.

"Mrs. A is a wonderful, warm, and extremely intelligent woman," I wrote, describing Bill's mom as witty but sick with worry, or inner strife. Woink had made an impression and I added that "poor Mrs. A just fell so in love with him." Catherine shared our concerns about the fate of humanity and our planet, so I told my parents: "She agrees with Bill, that this system won't hold, because most of what Bill says is in the Bible (tho he won't admit that his theories and moralistics have anything to do with the Bible)."

After Catherine and Andrew left, I wrote to them occasionally. Catherine encouraged me to stay in touch, partly because it connected her to Bill's world, but also because she had also taken an interest in me, and we had the beginning of a relationship that felt honest. During their visit I had seen that Bill was caring with his parents, and came to understand that he had a deep connection to them, especially his mother. It was revealing to see a part of Bill that was deferential, loving, and a little vulnerable. He was more guarded with his father, but I took that to be the chemistry between them, not something born of past grievances, and Bill would not have shared that with me in any case. Although I didn't know much about the dynamic between Bill and his older and younger brothers, he showed interest and concern about them. Bill and Catherine had talked at length about his younger brother, and when she'd shared her distress, asking Bill for his guidance, he had done his best to console her.

✕

CHAPTER TWENTY-NINE

*D*ad's birthday was the last day of September, so I sent a note a few days before that to say that he was special to me, I was grateful for his respect and understanding, and I wanted him to know that I loved him dearly—"more than a hundred times the number of stars at night. But more still . . ."

He wrote back right away.

Dearest Annie,

Your letter warmed my heart. Tho it needs no warming for you, you expressed the love we hold for each other. We needn't be maudlin about it but it never hurts to "tell it like it is."

Here, too, the days are turning from the heat of the green green green of summer to the golden hues of autumn. A quietness sets in —a sort of peace. The birds know it, the flowers show it and man feels it both within and without. Life itself should rest a bit before the rigors of winter place new demands on man and beast.

Mom and I are doing a different kind of preparing—that of seeing new lands, new people because albeit our lives are shortening not lengthening and there is so much to do and to see and to feel. Our horizons must stretch and quickly for too soon they may end. We all grow old but let not our youth die too soon.

You seem to have a gift for writing. Are you really making an

effort to put your own life on paper or can you draw it? I haven't
heard whether you are doing either. It is not enough to feed and ride
a pig or horse. Thousands—millions have done that before but
writers and painters of merit we have room for. Draw the pig. Write
deeply. Think BIG. Don't restrict your mind!!! If my counsel were
wanted, I would say to you; plan your life so that you have a variety
of experiences, meet many people and become as broad in scope as
possible. 5840 represents the beginning not the ending. Devote '75 to
another broadening. But think it through first. Then do it.
    Love you muchly
    Dad.

When I wrote to Mom and Dad on September 30, the
sun was rising at seven thirty, long after Chanticleer welcomed the morning. My days were busy with the usual
chores, and the last push of preparation for winter. I mentioned to them that we would be butchering Woink in a few
days, and would have to spend another few days after that
processing all the meat.

In answer to Dad's question about whether I had been
drawing or writing, I wrote, "I dread saying that I've been
poor at keeping a diary . . . oh, I write occasionally, but I
have such a hard time saying what I feel that I waste time
trying to put it down. And I can't bear to waste time when
so much needs doing. Time goes by so quickly that I lose
track of days & weeks even sometimes, and certainly this
life is not geared to watching a clock. I'll try to do some
drawings soon for you to give you an idea of this life."

It gnawed at me that I was not taking the time to nurture my own creative efforts. Even though I had been poking
along on the piano to learn the Rachmaninoff concerto when
Bill was not around to hear me, it was not very polished, and

not consistent enough to be fulfilling, so I only gave it a brief mention.

My sister had sent a letter, and I told my parents that she sounded happy. I asked them to tell her that I was proud of her and respected her, and mentioned that she was sweet and innocent, and maybe vulnerable because she was naïve. It was a disguised way to express concern for her. That thought shifted and I poured out a little homesick closing: "So we have a beautiful family—Dos is energy from the sun, Jen sparkling like a stream in the light, Geof, all heart and some nonsense, like a kid, and a young one who couldn't be happier about life, and who loves knowing there are always people like you two."

I included a request and list for Mom to send a box of supplies for winter, assuming a position of readiness for the months ahead, including scrap material so I could work on sewing a quilt:

* 8 pair wool socks

* Long Death

* Vit C & multiple

* Return of the King (or all of Tolkien's trilogy if possible) this is the 3rd book tho

* Vaseline intensive care lotion

* hair brush (should be a wooden one in my bathroom)

* Geof's address

* Wool pants (army/navy pants size 28 waist, 32 length-deep blue) if they fit you well Mom, they'll fit me—or Jen can get them if you don't have time

* Mukluks

a couple of Oral B 40 or 60 toothbrushes-

blue ball pt. pens (or black—Bill and I used & broke the other one working on the root house)

Wool shirts if you can find any, or heavy flannel button-downs— a little bigger than would fit you well Mom, or really whatever can hold long-johns underneath—same with wool pants

Scrap materials—any size shape, color

Asking Mom to send supplies for winter made me feel like a kid at camp, which didn't seem quite right. Wasn't I supposed to break free from home and take care of my own needs?

Suppertime had come and gone and it was almost dark when I heard the shots downstream. It made me uneasy because I didn't know what Bill was doing and it seemed late for hunting. He'd told me he was going out as he shouldered his gun, but by this time we were carrying on with our days more independently and I often didn't know where he was.

About an hour after I heard the shot, he yelled to me from outside to bring out a container. When I went out with a large bowl, he had a mass of soft, opaque material in his hands that he dropped into the pan. It looked like a white jellyfish lying there. He told me he had killed a black bear and had carried the leaf lard back so other critters would not be attracted to the carcass before we could get to it.

As soon as Bill cleaned up, we headed out on foot to retrieve the bear, which he said was about a mile or so downstream. The moon was bright and the crisp air penetrated our layers. Kriega, the white adult male cat, and two young cats, one grey, one white, followed us; they must have smelled the bear on Bill. Their coats were luminous in the full moonlight, and the evening unfolded in a dreamlike way.

As we approached the riverbank I could make out the dark form of the bear stretched out on the stones of the opposite bank, its feet in the water. Bill waded across, then hoisted the body—which must have been about equal in weight to his own—onto his shoulders in a fireman's carry. I felt a little useless as I watched him struggle to carry the bear back over the slippery stones. As we started for home, I tried to help steady and support some of the body that hung off his shoulder, but it was awkward and uncomfortable for Bill, so he decided we would have to get the truck to bring the bear back. We lowered it carefully to ground near the river at the edge of the woods, about a half mile from the cabin, and we walked back to the cabin to get the truck.

It was nearing midnight by the time we retrieved the bear and hung it with a pulley and rope above the barn door to keep it away from scavengers. We were exhausted and ready for bed.

In the morning we woke to a wet snow. While I started the fire, made breakfast, and did the chores, Bill removed the bear's heart and liver and brought them in for us to eat later that day, then went back out to gut the animal. As I worked in the cabin I could only watch some of that process from the kitchen window that faced the garage and pig pen, a dozen yards from the cabin. He cut the intestines out and put them aside to clean for sausage casings; that would be my job while he started the work to remove the hide from the body.

Skinning a bear is a surgical procedure, and Bill wielded his hand-hewn knives like a master chef. There is a layer of fat between the musculature and the hide, and he carefully cut through that layer with small slices as he worked the hide away from the body. Once the hide was free, he hung it up next to the naked bear.

The knives he'd forged from blanks (flat rectangles) of good steel were incredibly sharp. When I first arrived, he'd just been finishing a new knife. I'd watched intently as he held the steel over the fire, heating it until it glowed red hot (but not so hot that it melted or became brittle), then took it to the anvil to shape it with a special hammering tool. Once he had the shape he wanted, he allowed it to cool to the point where it was malleable enough to file and re-fine, and finally it emerged as a beautifully sculpted knife blade with a slight curve at the point for easing under and through hides and around bones. Bill carved the knife handles from elk antler, which is tough but not brittle, and wonderful to hold. On each handle he etched images of animals and birds of prey, making them both works of art and talismans.

The intestines were full of offal. I carried the heavy loops of soft material—like skinny water balloons—down to the river. Bill showed me how to clean them out, and it reminded me of milking the goats: just squeeze and keep squeezing, like getting the last of the toothpaste from the tube. It was a long process since there was about twenty-five feet of intestine, filled with whatever that bear had eaten and digested. I wondered about contamination of the water while emptying that fecal material into the river, but did what I was told. Once I had cleared out the offal, I held the end open and let the river water run in and through the intestines to thoroughly cleanse the inside.

After the intestines were clear and drained, I carried the empty, soggy mass to the outside tub, where Bill had set up a saltwater bath so they could soak for a couple of hours; this, he said, would kill any remaining bacteria. He told me to try to get as much of the warm, salty water into the intestines as I could, so I sloshed them and tried to coax the water into the wriggly mass, but I wasn't entirely sure if I got the water all the way through. I thought back to the pea-canning incident and hoped it wouldn't be an issue— but I didn't say anything.

Once they were clean, we had to lift them out of the bath together to empty the saltwater. Then Bill closed off one end to fill them with air, just like blowing up a balloon, so they would dry properly and be easier to work with when we started stuffing them with sausage meat. As he blew them up, they formed into two-foot loops, and we joked about their kinship with skinny circus balloons and the animal shapes you can twist them into. Bill wanted a photograph of the bear and intestines so I ran inside for my Instamatic camera and snapped a photo as he held the intestine balloons and posed next to the bear, which was still hanging naked in front of the garage, looking strangely human.

Bill with the skinned bear and cleaned intestines

With so many focused tasks, the day went by quickly. The bear's carcass and hide would hang overnight on the barn until the next day, when we would butcher and prepare the meat.

Once that was out of the way, Bill would soak the hide in brain-tanning mash, so we were free to rest that evening. As we ate the liver and heart that night I felt something akin to reverence, as if I would now be closer to the being of the bear.

The next day, as Bill cut the bear apart, I cleaned off the large work area in front of the window and set up the meat grinder. Since we couldn't possibly eat all of the meat while it was fresh, and he didn't want to can any of it, we would make sausage and prepare various cuts of meat for the smokehouse. Bill cut the bear into large sections to be smoked; shoulders, flanks, ribs, and haunches (hams). The rest we cut from the bone and put through the meat grinder, then added dried sage, marjoram, pepper, salt, oregano, savory, and cayenne and sent it through the grinder again and into the intestine casings, which we tied into three-foot lengths and looped for hanging in the smokehouse.

Bill taught me how to tie up the hams, shoulders, and flanks with twine, then we rubbed them with salt to help cure the meat. When we were done, they looked just like the hams from the butcher shop. After that, he prepared the smokehouse, a chamber shaped like an outhouse, with a fire pit at the bottom and racks above for hanging the meat.

It took several weeks to smoke larger cuts of meat. Once they were done, they'd keep for some time, since they were cured by the smoke in a chemical process that not only cooked but also preserved the meat. The sausage would be cured in a just a handful of days, and we looked forward to sampling the smoky flavorings.

Tanning the hide was another involved process. After Bill scraped the hide clean of the fat, he coated the fleshy side with a mixture of the bear's own mashed brains with some rotting deer brains that he kept in a large bucket, and he added wood ash to the mix. Brains are acidic, ash is basic, and together they break down the fibers of the tough hide. The mash was intensely aromatic because of the decay. Bill then rolled the hide and put it in an old bathtub outside, added the brain/ash mix and left it to soak in the solution for several days, until the tough fibers softened. After that, he tied up the whole hide, anchored it to the shore, and rinsed it for two or three days in the river. He then laced it, still wet, to the stretching rack, and worked it manually with a scraping tool to further break up the fibers. The final step was to smoke the hide to keep it from rotting, as some moisture and bacteria would still be left in the flesh after it air-dried.

A few weeks earlier, when I'd scraped a stretched deer hide, I'd gotten a feel for how arduous this process was. Bill was proud that he followed the same method that the Native Americans had, and in attempting it myself I gained a new appreciation for what Indians had done just carrying out their daily tasks.

It was October 4 when I next wrote home to thank Mom for sending photos of her completed portrait, and let her know that Bill and I were both impressed with it. He had even asked me to tell her so. I described the episode with the bear in my letter, including details about cleaning out the intestines and making the sausage. And I mentioned that Woink "acted like a frightened rabbit for a couple of days, but he's ok now. We kill him tomorrow anyway. Then when Woink yields his meat, oh boy!"

Since we had just butchered the bear, I had a good idea of that process, and although I didn't look forward to another two or three days of preparation, I knew I could handle it. But the thought of killing Woink made me edgy with dread, and I could not love him hard enough to dull that edge.

CHAPTER THIRTY

I felt close to Woink in a way that I never would have imagined. When I headed out the door to do the chores, he trotted behind me—into the barn to milk the goats, or to sit by the garden as I weeded. Sometimes he came into the shed outside the kitchen and pushed the door open to see if we were inside. The handful of times I straddled him and held on around his neck while he trotted a few steps, Bill and I laughed and hooted, but Woink was not amused. When we talked to him, he was attentive; he tilted his head and twitched his ears and he seemed to understand that we were including him. And he was always smiling; he brought light to Val Halla.

Woink seemed nervous when Bill brought the bear's body home. The smell of death must have been frightening; he acted jumpy and I thought I could see fear in his eyes. After a couple of days he settled down, but I knew he felt anxious. So did I. I hated the whole idea of killing Woink and dreaded the act itself because I was so afraid that he would suffer. As much as I tried to override my emotions, a knot of sorrow grew in the pit of my stomach.

I stayed quiet and masked my feelings, of course; I couldn't break down in front of Bill. He talked about Woink in terms of bacon: he'd bought the pig to raise for meat, and that was the pig's destiny. We needed the meat and lard, and couldn't have a pig for a pet: Woink ate lots of grain and didn't contribute a lick of work around the place. Bill enjoyed Woink as an animal companion as much as I did, but clearly he could separate his emotions from what needed to be done in a way I couldn't. I felt pretty sure that no matter how hard I tried not to, I would feel the same way with the next pig, and the one after that. In many ways, thinking about killing Woink made me doubt whether I could live this lifestyle for the long term.

In letters home to Mom and Dad about Woink, I wanted to be sure-footed: "Oh well, it is a job that must be done." But Mom sensed my underlying dread, and she was quietly sympathetic.

We knew which day was Woink's last. It might have been better not knowing, but we had to prepare. Bill would cut up the meat into hams, shoulders, loins, and sides to smoke. We would make sausage from the rest. Having processed the bear meat just the week before, I knew it would be another two-day task.

Bill and I had taken photos of each other with Woink the previous day. He always stayed near the cabin, lying in the sun or shade, so we each gave him a big hug and scratch under the chin and captured those hugs on film to remember him. It was as close to a loving farewell as I could imagine, and I was relieved at the way Bill exposed his heart.

That morning was beautiful and clear and warm. We started a fire outside in a pit near the garage where the bear had hung and set a fifty-five-gallon drum of water on the fire ring for dunking Woink's body in order to soften the roots of the stiff hairs before scraping them from his hide. Woink was lying in the sun, just where we had photographed him the day before. Bill was calm and had let me know his plan: he would use his new knife and kill Woink with a blow to the heart. He carefully felt Woink's ribs to find the place where he could slip a knife between them and into his chest. I was glad he wasn't going to club him or shoot him or slit his throat; it felt more peaceful and honorable to simply stop his heart.

Bill went into the cabin and came back out with a rifle. He handed it to me and told me to stand nearby and shoot Woink in case he missed the heart and Woink started to run. I was more afraid of my role if that happened than just about anything I had experienced at Val Halla to that point. It meant that if Bill failed, I would have to kill Woink, and he would be terrified and in pain. I prayed to whatever gods that Woink would die easily.

When we were ready Bill approached Woink without hesitation. I stood about eight feet away with the rifle. Bill kneeled next to him, surveyed the point of entry and the direction of the heart, and thrust the blade in. It was clean and fast: Woink squealed and jumped up, then stumbled and fell, and he was gone. It happened as I had prayed it would.

We dragged Woink over to the drum of hot water, tied his hind feet, and used pulleys to hoist him up into the air high enough to then lower him into the boiling water. After a minute or two we lifted his body out and lay him on the ground so Bill could cut him open. At that point he was an anatomy lesson for me. It is truly amazing to look inside a creature to see all the parts that make us into living, sentient beings. We could see the path of the knife and the inch-deep wound in the heart that made Woink stop.

Again we ate the heart and liver fresh that day. The blood in his lungs had congealed from the hot water and we even ate some of that, fried as you would a slice of liver. Like the bear, it felt like a way to keep a part of Woink with me.

Later that day I cut the meat from Woink's head to make a pork pot pie. While I cut into the thick, fleshy hide from around his head I kept picturing the day before, when he had been poking around the yard with the goats and chickens—and now here he was, becoming a pot pie, his eyes looking into space. I wanted to talk to him, to tell him I would miss him; as I cut away the layers around the snout and scull and eyes, however, I was also fascinated by how all the bones and muscles of a pig's head fit together.

The pot pie was one of the best dishes I ever made at Val Halla. But I couldn't stop thinking about Woink. Pigs are sensitive and bright, and maybe even curious. I had connected deeply with our wonderful pig, and now that he was gone I felt so empty. Woink had been a true source of joy and levity, and that had disappeared with him.

A loving hug, Woink's last day

CHAPTER THIRTY-ONE

*M*om wrote a note on Sunday, October 6, to let me know that she had collected most of the items on my list and would be sending along a box, but without any newspaper for packing materials since she assumed we had kindling. She and Dad were getting ready for a trip to Europe to spend time with Dad's brother-in-law in Spain and explore parts of France, and they would be gone for over a month. She urged me to write to my sister or my brother, Dos, who would be house-sitting for them, since they would keep the letters for her and Dad to read at a later date, and she added, "don't worry about keeping a diary as your letters are a diary. By the way, please date them as the postmark is quite often smudged."

On Tuesday, October 8, I put a letter in the box for Mom and Dad while Mom's note was still en route. I let them know that Woink had died painlessly with "a deadly blow from Bill's knife through the heart." I then described the process of scalding, scraping, gutting, and butchering him, and the next steps to prepare the sausage and the cuts of meat to smoke. We sampled some of the sausage fresh before we hung the loops in the smokehouse with the hams, and I described it to my parents:

> *Best sausage I ever ate—the first batch we seasoned with sage, salt,*
> *pepper (black & cayenne) marjoram, etc—and it's pretty hot, spicy*

—the second batch we ground up mint & dried huckleberries, salt, some sage, allspice & pepper—mild and flavorful! Last batch is seasoned with chili powder, salt, pepper & tastes rather Mexican, a fine flavor & should be delicious smoked. We've cooked some spare ribs too, oh Woink was a good friend, but he's sure good eatin'! We even saved his clotted blood, and fried, it tastes much like liver, only more tender and with a very delectable taste—if you get a chance, ask the butcher to get you some, really it's good stuff, and more nutritious than any meat you could buy!

I was happy for them to travel but had relied on their letters like a beacon from the shore, so the idea that I might be without them for a time made me feel lost. Cini had just sent a letter and asked me if I ever missed home and wanted to come back, and the simple answer was yes. But it was deeper and more complicated and I was still weighing what it meant to go home against what I would have to do to stay at Val Halla. In my letter to Mom and Dad I pushed all of my options into the open, hoping they would help me sort the feelings, fears, and goals. They couldn't help with my fraying dynamic with Bill, but it was time to measure my commitment, and I had to decide on his behalf as well. Even though we were still sleeping together, our sexual encounters were passionless. There was no love that could soften the hard times, and I missed the love and comfort of family and friends.

Bill showed his aggravation when I didn't meet his expectations, but it was broader than single incidents, and growing into something we both felt but couldn't resolve. I exposed this to my parents and opened up to show them the disarray of my heart. I shared, "Maybe I'm expecting too much because I'm not participating enough, it's just that I'm not trying as hard as I ought to really become a part of this life, and that annoys & aggravates Bill, and he cuts deep, and that makes me less willing to try. So, something is wrong here. I'm pulling Bill's spirit down, at the same time his remarks and attitude about things that touch my life certainly are cutting and often unnecessary."

The beauty, the freedom, and the lifestyle of Val Halla still seemed ideal to me, and I wanted to be the tough girl who could ride a horse, handle the workload, and immerse myself wholeheartedly in that world. It had been my goal to become self-reliant, but I was not living up to my own expectations, and it felt terrible.

In my letter I admitted that I was not learning enough, not paying attention, not taking advantage of all that Bill was willing to teach me, and I was worried that coming home would be the unhappy result of that failure. I was still thinking that I might be able to spend the winter, if things with Bill improved, and wrote, "since I've always claimed that this is what I truly wanted, I'd damned sure better try and show myself some guts and go at it, girl, or else the spirit may die." Hoping to show some determination, I scolded myself on paper. "Well enough of this self pity act, I'm just upset in feeling the backfire of too much carelessness, not enough appreciation and a welling sense of failure. You said I wouldn't have failed to return home; little do you know that that's exactly what it would be—to have to get a job or go to school, to just become another puppet of the system. But I do recognize good, and want to do good. I am simply confused."

There was a chance that I could recreate the lifestyle for myself somewhere, some day, and I held on to that thought as a way to release myself from Bill's realm. I was convinced that it was critical to live an off-the-grid, self-sufficient lifestyle, telling my parents, "the system will fold, the depression, perhaps universal famine will come, and this is good preparation for it."

And I was afraid of calling it quits, equivocating on paper that I should just try harder, learn as much as I could, and stay through winter with Bill, feeling as if I had not really pushed to endure or discover what that life could offer. I exposed that I was feeling dull and empty, and wrote, "so I'll try and see if I succeed—okay by you?" And closed my letter, "Well, I've not lost heart, but do miss you both so much. Much much love, Annie."

By the time my parents received my letter, it was mid-October, and Dos had sent it on to them in Spain. Dad answered with his heart.

Dearest Annie,

Mom and I got your thoughtful and provoking letter which Dos forwarded to us here.

First and foremost, you, Annie, have all the love that we as parents can bestow upon you and I think we certainly feel your love for us. Further our whole desire is for both the wellbeing and happiness of our children. But we want those things to be long range and to be constructive and not just for immediate pleasure. So you have written to us that your life there with Bill lacks perhaps what we all seek and want most—LOVE. Not in the sexual sense, but in the sense of understanding, mutual compatibility, respect and mutual regard of one another.

I hold to the view I have expressed before that you have done or tried hard to do what you set out to do and it would be no defeat, no deceit for you to look toward another approach. Life is made up of changes both in living and in thinking and I feel you still have much to learn and feel about other people and other places.

What does coming home mean? Well, to me coming home would only mean coming in order to accept whatever guidance and reassurance we could give you for a new going forward, because life itself is a going forward to new learning and to new growth and a seeking of that better love of moral and spiritual fulfillment. That, my dear love, is what I feel. You have a great deal to give and I think your giving and receiving now can best be shared by former friends and new ones not yet known.

We have had a very satisfying time helping Cuz in Spain. After all he is going forward. He must reconnoiter and make new friends and find a new way too!

I love you very much
Dad.

When I read Dad's letter, I felt relieved. Mom and Dad didn't see me as a failure, and they were urging me to grant that understanding for myself. I appreciated that Dad saw a path for me that included support, love, and opportunity. The door cracked open, and I had to decide if I would go through.

CHAPTER THIRTY-TWO

*G*reen, gold, and blue curtains of light were cascading down through the night sky as Bill and I stood transfixed, entertained by the spectacular Aurora Borealis. The evening was chilly; a late-October cold warned us that winter was on its way. Over and over I had played out in my mind what winter would bring. The cold and snow would present certain challenges in tending to the animals and dealing with hauling water, food preparation, cleaning, and keeping the cabin warm. I imagined long, dark months with the sewing, beading, and drawing projects I was planning, and looked forward to immersing myself in those quiet meditations.

But those comforting dreams were overshadowed by uneasiness and fear and an urge to leave and retreat to the comfort of home before the snow arrived. I was not as sturdy as I thought I would be—was afraid of the trials of winter and anxious about extended indoor time with Bill. The life I was living was one of choice—a world that I could enter like a theater, and leave at intermission if I wanted to. Bill had warned me in letters that the lifestyle I longed for was not a play. What would it take to become the strong, independent woman I thought I could just step into, like a character in Laura Ingalls Wilder's stories? The reality of my weakness stung like the heartache of loss. Once or twice Bill accused me of being a dilettante, and it was true.

By now my thoughts were clear and I knew it was time to leave. I understood that my relationship with Bill would never grow to be the kind of bond that makes living with another person joyous. He had hinted that he was not easy with the notion of my staying, and I had the sense that I should make a decision before it was made for me. So, as the northern light rained down, I told Bill I would be leaving the next day. He gently agreed that it was best, and then we stood quietly.

I was so young and so uncertain, and I'd never known how to feel comfortable around Bill. I was sorry that I was not the right partner for him, especially knowing he'd been hurt so deeply when Helen left Val Halla, but we had enjoyed a few adventures. He'd appreciated some of what I had been able to accomplish, especially in the food department (aside from the canned-pea debacle). And we had gotten into a comfortable routine on most days, where the chores, the beauty of the river and peaks, and the simple pleasures of growing food and tending the animals was enough. He had been more than generous in sharing his time, experience, resources, and that sacred corner of his world with me. I, meanwhile, had worked hard to try to fit into his world, and hoped that I'd returned that gift with some of my own offerings and compassion. Although neither of us expressed it, I think we were both grateful to have shared the time we did.

Joe and Flo and I had already talked about my leaving earlier that day. They had been at their little cabin for a day or two when I walked across the meadow to visit. Flo, in all her wisdom, had known what was in my heart and had not been a bit surprised when I told them I thought it best to leave before winter settled in. They would take me to their home in Bigfork, where I could stay a few days before going back to Denver. They had both watched carefully as I made my way through the summer with Bill. They'd acted as my guardians without ever interfering, and I felt a deep comfort in their honesty and concern for me, and for Bill.

Sometime before supper the next day, Joe and Flo drove across the meadow to help me finish packing and say good-bye to Bill. I was inside finishing up with some chores while Bill was out visiting with a girl my age whose family had rented the fishing cabins that summer, and a couple of her friends from the University of Montana.

Leaving Bill was just as awkward as arriving had been; we were friendly, yet there was an unbridgeable distance. When we embraced and said goodbye, there wasn't the res-onance of friends who hope for a next visit. How could I share what was in my heart? My face flushed and I had little to say; I tried to express thanks, but it felt inade-quate. Bill reflected my uneasiness. He chatted a bit with Joe and Flo while I gathered my duffel, packing Teddy in among my clothes, but he was not his usual, talkative self. He may have been wary of judgments being passed, and guarding his world from the intrusion of three-dimensional emotion. Still, we respected one another, and there was no residue of upset. When we got into the car, he leaned into the driver's side and thanked Joe and Flo for taking good care of me.

The ride down the dirt road toward the valley was quiet. Joe and Flo allowed me those couple of hours for my soul to settle.

The knotty-pine walls and ruffled curtains in Joe and Flo's cabin-like home in Bigfork soothed me like an elixir of comfort and happiness. Flo put me into the bath almost as soon as we got to the house and even reminded me to wash behind the ears—I felt like a kid in a Norman Rockwell painting. Sponge baths and showers at the cabin had always felt good, but the hot water immersion of a real bath was heavenly.

Flo washed all of my clothes twice, since once didn't do it. Washing clothes in cold water by hand had not done the job, at least not by modern standards; when you live apart from washing machine convenience, you don't notice being less than aseptic and spotless.

Flo told me they were glad that I "got smart" and left Bill as soon as I did, adding that they were fond of him but . . . Her phrasing indicated that there was a long story behind their comment, but I didn't press for details.

That night we called Dos at my parents' house to let him know I would be home in a few days. In the meantime, Joe and Flo helped me ease back into the world. Joe took me on a tour of the firehouse where he had been captain, and we toured the small hydropower station in Bigfork where he was the foreman; we stood right over the turbines and felt the rumble, mesmerized by the water dropping into giant funnels. Flo showed me photos of her family and cooked warming meals. We watched the birds at their feeders and went to their special spot at Soup Creek for a picnic.

After four days, I was ready to go home to Denver. Dos would be there to greet me at the airport and stay at the house with me, and I would just have to fit back into my old life as best I could. In some ways I looked forward to using my new skills, especially cooking. I felt stronger, and pleased that I had not missed smoking pot and the idea of drinking hadn't even occurred to me while I'd been at Val Halla.

On a more subtle level, I now understood solitude and felt more comfortable with spending time alone. But I was not sure how I would meet other challenges, like finding a job or being a useful citizen in a new way, or how well I could integrate back into the social and privileged world that lay under my parents' roof.

CHAPTER THIRTY-THREE

*A*s I expected, adjusting to being home was a challenge. Before I even left Montana, when I called my sister to let her know I was coming home, she said my brother-in-law would be happy to fly up to Kalispell to pick me up in a small plane. I told her that I would prefer to fly commercially. The last thing I needed was to have to deal with his overtures before I even got myself back home.

A day or two later, on October 28, I sent a letter to Mom and Dad from Denver. Dos and I had already called them in Spain to let them know I was home and fine. The letter touched on the dissolving situation with Bill, and explained how Joe and Flo had helped me when it was time to leave Val Halla and let me stay with them for a few days.

Mom and Dad wrote back right away, relieved and happy that I was home. After all of their concern about me over the past year, I was glad that my situation was no longer a dark cloud hanging over them, and I imagined them touring the countryside, visiting sights and sharing roadside picnics, with lighter hearts.

The noise and city life felt invasive after so much quiet time away and I was having trouble sleeping. But I stayed busy with cleaning and cooking and working out a diet and exercise plan with my brother, since we both had extra weight to lose. Bill's birthday was the first week of November, and I bought some beads to make a new headband for him; I wanted to let him know that I appreciated my time at Val Halla, and would not lose touch with that life, or him.

Only a few people knew I was home—I was hesitant to engage in any social life—but Dos and I did visit my grandparents, and it was nice to be around family again. I spent lots of time with Cini and her folks, who wanted to hear all my stories about life with Bill at Val Halla. Once or twice while I was hanging out with Cini at the Carsons' house, Hollis stopped by and we had a chance to share our Montana experiences. When I went down to their gallery to visit, I put a down payment on one of Bill's engravings of an eagle in an elk ivory medallion that I admired, happy that I would have some of his artwork. There were also some lovely framed charcoal drawings of a mountain man that Hollis had done; beautiful finished artwork that he'd made from his sketches of Bill while he visited with us. All of these connections reminded me of the passion I still had for that remote world.

With so much free time, and no Bill watching over my shoulder, I felt more relaxed about trying my hand at engraving. I etched the image of a rabbit for a friend in a piece of a deer antler, and an owl in another piece of antler for Lana, who had visited with Ken at Val Halla. Now that I didn't have to worry about anyone judging my work, it felt good to immerse myself in small, creative projects.

When I finished the headband for Bill, just in time for his thirty-fourth birthday, I was pleased with it. The blue, orange, red, and black geometric pattern of arrows and zigzag lines was striking, and I was excited to send it to him, along with a small supply of string, safety pins and pencils, and some other items he might need. The idea that we could stay in touch and on good terms helped ease the lingering sorrow I felt over leaving him.

My connection to the wilderness realm at Val Halla was a valuable part of my life, and I worried that it might fade with time. I started thinking about visiting Bill once we'd both had time to settle into new patterns for ourselves. As difficult as it had been for us to navigate a future together, I never thought that he wanted me out of his life forever, and I hoped that with space, we could create a different kind of connection. My experience there had been so intense, and was still fresh, but it was not clear to me what emotions I was juggling. In my journal I expressed that it felt like love without longing, writing, "I only wish that I could write him and tell him my feelings—but he would never take me seriously, or he would resent them, I know. He's just that way."

When I did write to him, I simply shared news about Hollis and the Carsons, my small projects, the weather, and whatever I thought might sound interesting.

Bill sent a handwritten letter back, dated November 8, in which he was surprisingly kind, even caring.

USED YOUR SCALPEL BLADE TO REMOVE 3 STITCHES This Night.

Annie Gal,

Received the box of needed gifts. They will come in handy. Don't know where you found the Hydro Cortisone, damn sharp to remember. I like the headband. The colors & the design will look good with buckskins & fur. You hurried on it, didn't you.

Just ate 3 Woink Chops, spuds & turnips & fried apples. I'm down to a week of fresh Woink meat. You missed some of the finest eating this side the Great Divide. It has kept perfectly for weeks

Due to no rain or snow yet. It has held in Indian Summer all month. But the skies tonight are heavy with snow.

Everything is done for the Ghost Face to mantle the world of Val Halla. Hunting elk is the main chore now. Took Ahkee and made a big circle of the hunting grounds. Elk are there—found much sign & dozens of saplings stripped of bark. Some so fresh, only hours old. I know where a bull comes each night to bed down. Going to try & get a look at him if he's magnificent enough, need antlers for the bedroom window.

Trucked all the extra dirt & debris away from the sides of the root house & covered the old dump. The cellar looks like a Mandan Earth lodge now. 2 days smoked it with juniper, and what a delicious smell to go down into. Built the shelves and carried all canned goods down while working on elk hide. Soft as cashmere it is. Had 2 hard spots so put brains to it again. The 2 halves of calf elk I've brained a 3rd time, but it will be superb when done. The secret is to leave it in brains long enough. With rotten pig brains, and rotten bear brains, and a quart of rotten deer brains, GOD WHAT A PUTRID SMELL. But the buckskin is snow white and going to be the softest there is. It wouldn't do but to have a suit of elk skins this winter.

And the smell of cherry smoked hams & bacon is something to savor. 3 times a day a few chunks of wood and she slow smokes day after day. All night for over two weeks now, maybe 3. And that delicious smell. I wish to smoke some buckskin with some as the sweet smell is too good.

Got an elk head found in the woods. The brains for the bear hide. I've figured a way to do robes to softest velvet, if I can get a couple of dozen heads. The Indian had unlimited skulls of buffalo for brains to do the finest hides & robes. If one spot is too thick &

doesn't dissolve all the glue, just soak it in brains a few days & work it again. Case your interested.

Sliced the heel of my hand open sharpening the butcher knife to cut the 1st bacon. Did 3 stitches immediately, Dental floss. Healed now.

Ahkee disappeared & I found horse tracks North in Canada. Fearing someone would try to steal him, I saddled & rode North. Found the horses, but Ahkee was gone, tracks North. Ahkee's moon feet. So, a rider was taking him North. Tracks showed he didn't slow or graze. Found him at McDougals. IMPOUNDED. But I changed saddles from Jere & tore out of there on Ahkee. Free to the wind. Took unknown trails to get far from roads, wound way up in the ridges South & East. Then it got so thick, had to lead them. Had to push trees & pull them over so thick to go through. Sun going down. Miles from the valley floor. Down, down we crashed. Hearing trickle water, finally the creek. One mile from the trail over the ridge to the river. And Home, at Dusk's teeth with a cold wind blowing. Val Halla.

Beaver traps are out. Ice forming fast. Two pelts needed. Prehaps an otter will chance into one trap. Days END.

Two elk hides soften Golden Smoky buckskin. Big bear hide being drug around field to check traps—hair side down, for the dew to "comb" it clean. Satin sheen shining already. A little more work & done then to smoke with the last of cherry wood. Big white throat & chest spotted mink back in traps. Beautiful to see. Frank came. Brought good news. Found an old farmhouse with 2 30-gallon crocks. He had one & said he'd get 2nd one for me when [he] comes in spring with canoe.

Jumped big herd elk. No chance for shot wind changed &

away they went. Washed heavy buckskin shirt. Like brand new.
Softest buckskin imaginable. 3 washings to clean.

 Ben & Marion were by. Marveled at root house & the raised
barn.

 The world is humming with the dread of hunger. Listen
carefully tomorrow.

 p.s. Your brave & strong to face the howling throng.
Will of the Wisp William

I could clearly picture the scenes that Bill described and I missed so much of what I had loved at Val Halla: waking up to Chanticleer crowing, leaning my head into Mia's side while I milked her, the smoky heat of the wood-stove, and the ambiance of the rustic cabin. I had been an integral part of a world where everything mattered—where every small task was key to the function of the whole in a tangible way that I had some role in, where small measures of success like making delicious bread or riding a horse without fear were enormously satisfying. My experiences with Bill had given me the strength to face the next challenges more readily, and I was starting to understand more about my capacity and abilities, limits, and fears.

✗

CHAPTER THIRTY-ONE

*E*ven as I held tight to the memory of Val Halla and tried to apply lessons learned there, I had wandered back into a life I'd wanted to leave behind, and I felt lost. The world of commerce and technology made me anxious and critical, and that became an issue. I would find myself in a retail store and say something outright rude about the glut of stuff, which seemed so superfluous, or I would comment widely to anyone in my path on the stupidity of careless waste. Mom and Dad were back from their trip and we enjoyed being together, but I couldn't undo my agitation, and at times it was directed at them. I chastised Mom for not scraping clean the eggs from their shells, or for throwing away an item I perceived as something with value: a scrap of material, an empty container. I knew logically that I had no control over the world outside my door and that I was unfairly punishing my family for the way they lived, but I was pushing back against this world that I had rejected in my longing for an alternative.

I tried to fill my time, but most activities held less than enough purpose since they were not directly related to subsistence. Mom and Dad felt my uneasiness and it frustrated them. As Mom watched my attempts to learn how to quilt, or my practical but disinterested foray into auto mechanics, she would urge me to get involved in something bigger than myself. We were irritable with each other on occasion, and our spats made me feel like an empty glass; they added to an already uncomfortable sense that I had left a dream behind and reality did not match my ideals of how the world should be. It was harder to steer myself in a realm of so much choice.

Mom understood, and made every effort to let me know she trusted that I would find my way; her concern and love provided a home. Dad was steady in urging me to get on with life—to go to school, find a focus, and concentrate on becoming a contributing member of society. His unwavering attitude helped me more than I could understand at the time. It was my job to fill in the blanks.

Bill's mother, Ken, and Lana all wrote after I left Val Halla, each offering that although I had not become the partner for Bill that I had envisioned, my time there had been important, a show of strength. Flo stayed in touch and chatted about trips to the North Fork, Joe's volunteer fire chiefdom, their grown kids and grandkids, picnics at Soup Creek, and local tidbits of gossip. Her voice jumped right off the page; I could hear her as clearly as if we were at the kitchen table sharing cookies and tea. She assured me that I had done my best. She didn't mince words, and said quite bluntly that I had given it my all and didn't owe Bill.

Of course, these were her thoughts. Flo had a much deeper history with Bill than I did, and my experience with him had been mostly positive. I was careful to filter out some of what she and others said about him.

On Christmas Day 1974, after a little celebration with my parents in the morning, I flew to Nebraska to stay a few days with my friend Marcia from Emma Willard. She was a shoulder I could rest my head on, and her levity and lack of judgment provided a respite from my inner dialogue. I had spent a little time with Marcia's parents and younger sister and loved their family dynamic; it was wholesome, fun-loving, and easy, and I craved that emotional tonic. The physical distance from home gave me a rest from the struggle of trying to reenter that world, and the persistent loops playing in my mind about Val Halla.

It wasn't until February that I'd receive another letter from Bill. In it, he told me about a woman who had arrived in his life who seemed to fit into the place I had dreamed about.

Feb 11, 1975

Dear Annie,

Hail, hail from the land of frozen ice and snow where the wolf rules supreme . . . wild and free. And so it is still, the world of Val Halla, but not silent anymore. A friend brought along a friend for a visit, and it appears this wild wild world of strengths and vigorous tasks is very agreeable to her. The world of scholarships and token honors and straight A grades quickly paled when stacked next to a world of beaver, bear, lion, moose, elk and deer. And HORSES. She, a lover of horses since a small child, but never once knowing what a freedom is felt from leaping upon a war horse and tearing off into the wilds.

Not exactly a deaf mute, but very quiet at times. We seem to know the heart of the dream made real beyond belief . . . and what it will take to create it in its entirety. She doesn't know if she can be

the one strong enough to take to the high trail . . . but that is the
goal, and Annie gal, I hope and hope and hope.

After that introduction to the new chapter in his life,
Bill wrote out a long description of his afternoon adventure
out on snowshoes, or "snow slippers" as he liked to call
them, checking his traps for otter. They turned up empty
but he crossed the frozen North Fork river and kept heading north into Canada to scout for elk sign, moving fast to
fight off the bitter cold. I shivered to think about facing
that biting cold, far from home, because the cold was one
element that I truly feared. After a short, surprising ride on
a small avalanche, he came on a pair of mountain lions who
did not detect him from one hundred and fifty yards away,
and he started to freeze but watched as they moved away
and disappeared. On his way home he met a cow moose and
her calf, but they turned and moved away from him.

He mentioned that he had received a letter from his
"little mother" a day or two earlier. "She said you had written a nice letter to them. And that the eagle engraving is
now your own. You never told me you liked that one." Then
he opened some of his heart to me, but only far enough to
get a glimpse of his feelings about our time together, and he
closed with his warnings about the world I had just stepped
back into.

I have purposely left off writing, little girl, to give you the break
you needed from this silent world of make believe and time to find
what your world of glittering lights and constant music holds once
again. I told you one has to be very very strong to walk out of that
world and survive, both mentally and physical wise. Now, prehaps
you believe me. We had some beautifully real moments together . . .

most of which no one will believe you could see in 1974. But, remember, this child has lived beyond the sight and sound of the mechanical materialistic world and its artificialdom until I no longer grasp its utter dependency on others to survive. Annie, take a good look at what is in store for this country if it doesn't "Capture" oil reserves soon . . . Remember my 11 positive points? Seems I mentioned then what was about to transpire.

Remember, Annie. To be really free, you must never allow a single fear to enter in . . . for once a root fear takes hold, the tree grows and grows. Be strong. Watch with wolf's eyes ever alert, ever wary, ever wild.

The Crazy Wolf

Bill's announcement about another woman landing in his life so soon left me feeling hollow. I read and reread his opening description about her, amazed that she had stepped in to fill the role I had hoped to assume. Bill seemed so complete, and softened in a way I had only mused about. And yet I was grateful that he could share his news with me, as if he was writing to a sister or a friend he trusted, and some of my initial upset dissipated at my recognition of what seemed like a new relationship with him. I was curious about this woman who could enter into Bill's life and adjust to feel at home so immediately, and I wanted to meet her. I wrote to Bill right away and said that I hoped she would be strong and help him create the loving world he imagined. And I told him I would not give up my search for a life apart from the burdens of society, and that I was not afraid.

My unstructured time at home without larger goals was wearing all of us down, and Mom and Dad suggested I go to the cabin for a few days with Josie to sort out some thoughts, spend some time away from them, and adjust my sour attitude. It was a good idea. Now that I had a car, I could go alone, shop for my own groceries, and take care of myself. It would be cold at the cabin, but the big woodstove in the kitchen would keep us warm and I now had the skills to cook my own meals.

Josie and I headed out of Denver and up to the cabin on February 13, just before the coming weather set in. As soon as we got there, I unpacked the groceries, split some kindling, and got the fire started in the woodstove. It was a comfortable routine, and I was happy to feel independent and capable again.

The next morning, we woke to a steady snowfall. It was a gorgeous picture-book scene, with every branch and shrub frosted with a coating of snow. When I went out to the woodpile with Josie, only the frozen lake ice, with its booming and groaning, resounded below the intense quiet. After a walk and some woodpile chores, we settled into the rest of the day at the kitchen table near the heat of the woodstove; I wrote in my journal and did some drawing while the kettle hummed and a pot of beans simmered on the stove.

My journal entry, dated February 15, only touched on Bill's letter about his new situation; it focused more on thoughts about a note that Bill's mother, Catherine, had sent in answer to my letter to her about trying to find a way to fit back into my old life. My entry was brief but alluded to her thoughts about what religious faith would offer. I didn't trust organized religion, or indoctrination, but I was curious. "Maybe his mother is right," I wrote. "She says that I am going in the right direction—but if I were to put my faith in God, then I would be peaceful inside, and be able to face any circumstance without fear."

Anxiety and frustration were taking over; I was exhausted by it and wanted to fill my inner landscape with better stuff. But religion had never really made much sense to me. I thought that the tenets of being a decent human should be part of everyone's playbook, and that adhering to a certain God and rulebook according to societal norms only caused problems on a number of levels. Inner peace sounded good, but I just couldn't all of a sudden adopt faith in God. I was much more interested in Buddhist philosophy, even though I didn't know much about it.

Over the next few days, while I spent time reading, writing, and drawing, I searched for what it was I did believe and could use as a guide to help settle my fears, set my own positive path, and pursue a life that I could tolerate, or even use to make a contribution to the world. I eased back into drawing and sketching, and enjoyed the total concentration as I tried to capture the Born woodstove in a pencil drawing, the glass vase full of old spoons on the table, and the rock spires of the Castle looming above the lake out the kitchen window, on paper. I had recently picked up *The Zen of Seeing*, by Friedrick Franck, and was interested in his loose gesture sketches drawn alongside notes about the drawing. He expressed his thoughts about taking the world in and truly "seeing" it with his pen as a meditation for living in the moment. And it was true. The world slowed to a pace that I met with simple, deep observation, and time seemed to shift into a different gear. It felt like I had entered a place I had been looking for. I wanted to pay attention and try to understand the experience. I wrote in my journal:

When I draw, I guess that I do not draw what I feel—but draw and overdraw too much of what I think the object looks like. Now, after reading The Zen of Seeing I feel like I never really "saw" or "see" what I am looking at. So now I know why I never feel right about a drawing that is too exacting—because it lacks feeling, insight—I did not "inscape" into the object but looked down on it as a thing. Also, when successful, there was the ego, the ME that shone above all, and then the picture lost its mystique, its true beauty, because I tried to shine above it, as the artist. But really, the scene, person, animal, makes the hand see, makes the heart feel, and become one with the drawing. Zen Buddhism is a pure unadulterated form of Seeing/Feeling, and Seeing/Drawing in its expression.

CHAPTER THIRTY-FIVE

*B*y March I still felt entirely out of place and couldn't figure out a job or other ways to stay busy. Mom and Dad were anxious for me to get on with my life, and I just couldn't stay at home, so I planned a month-long driving trip, heading first to meet up with Lana in Arizona, since she would join me for part of the trip. From there we'd head for the coast of California, where I could visit my brother, Geof, and his wife in Berkeley. Then I'd drive Lana all the way up to Vancouver, BC, drop her off with friends, and head east over the mountains to visit Bill and meet his new mate, Laurie, at Val Halla, as well as Joe and Flo in Bigfork, before heading home.

Lana and I had been writing to each other regularly. She seemed to understand the displacement I'd felt since leaving Montana, and wanted to spend time with me on the road. My parents understood that I had to set my own course but were concerned that I was adventuring without much road experience, so they set me up with phone numbers, maps, and emergency supplies for my car before I left.

During this time, I'd applied to Colorado College. My mom's younger sister had attended there in the '40s, and it seemed like a place I would fit into: only seventy miles away from Denver, and small enough to be negotiable. I had not even gone to visit the college—I'd just sent in my application fee and four handwritten essays, and that was that. Mom and Dad were encouraged that at least I was choosing a more moderate path.

This was my first long road trip; the adventure presented a new challenge, as I was an inexperienced driver, and I was a little nervous about all the unknowns. On April 8, I set my course southwest, toward New Mexico.

At dusk, as I was heading west out of Santa Fe, the mesas stood black against a scarlet, orange, and deep blue sky, and the clouds opened up in a fan shape on either side of the sun as I drove, almost as though I had my own special pathway to the sky.

After dark it became a strain to drive, so I decided to stop near Albuquerque, an hour or so away. But when a huge jackrabbit jumped in front of the car and I had to swerve to miss it, I pulled off the highway and onto a small dirt road, hoping to find a place to stop and sleep. I drove right into an old cemetery, however, and that seemed ominous, so I didn't stay there but kept going. I finally found a campground in a small town near the Rio Grande; I pulled in there and set up my sleeping bag in the back of my car, and crawled in. It had been a long first day.

The next morning I drove through parts of the Navajo Nation, and it was odd to see the southwestern landscape marred with myriad billboards advertising handmade Indian moccasins, beadwork, and suggestions to take a teepee home. Heading west toward Arizona, I crossed a mountain range near Flagstaff and passed through a tall, thick ponderosa pine forest where new snow blanketed the ground and trees. The road wound down the other side and into a valley pierced with tall cactus and palm trees, air scented by orange groves—a desert wonderland. It was exciting and liberating to simply navigate and watch the scene change as I drove.

Toward the end of the day, I finally arrived in Mesa, Arizona, where I found Lana home at her mother's trailer. We talked into the night and left the next day for California.

Conversation with Lana was easy, but she often drifted into thoughts about her own world, and didn't seem to grasp a sense of my reality. Her answer to everything was to just be cool, and life would sort itself out. After she and I parted ways in Vancouver a week or so later, I was glad to be on my own. She was *so* laid back on our adventure that I had been frustrated at times. I tried to slow down to meet her pace—to relax about details and practice being in the moment—but she seemed intentionally naïve, and something about it came across as forced. I was eager to get to Montana and visit Laurie and Bill, so my patience with Lana was thin, but we parted on good terms.

Going back to Val Halla as a visitor determined the energy of this journey. I felt none of the nervous fear of the unknown, or the sorrow buried in the underlying need to escape from a situation. It was Bill's Val Halla, and with Laurie there, I imagined I wouldn't need to try to make their world my own. Bill was writing to me as a friend now, and our relationship no longer held expectation or the ever-present wariness and criticism that had shadowed my time with him.

Without the distraction of Lana's company, I let my mind slip into a quiet mode of picturing the cabin, barn, animals, and landscape of Bill's home, and the anticipation of a reunion. Driving alone was the ideal space to immerse myself in thoughts about my path ahead as well, but nothing very certain formed in my mind, so I allowed myself to wander.

The drive from Seattle over Snoqualmie Pass toward Spokane was terrifying: a blizzard obscured the road, so I was relieved to be behind a snowplow for most of the trip down the eastern side of the pass. When I finally got to Missoula after twelve hours of driving, I stayed the night with a friend in her dorm at the university there, grateful to have a place to land.

It was nearing the end of April when I finally drove up to Val Halla the next day. The snow was still deep, but the road was plowed for the logging trucks.

When he heard my car as I pulled in near the cabin, Bill came out. He gave me a big bear hug in greeting. Laurie was right behind him, and she wrapped her arms around me, offering an incredibly warm welcome given that we had never met. Even though Laurie, who called herself "Little Fawn," had been with Bill for only a few months, she was comfortable and happy that I had come to visit. And Bill seemed relaxed and lighter. Then Ken stepped out of the cabin. I was happy to see him but not so surprised, since he had mentioned his plan to come back to Val Halla for an extended visit when he was with us over the summer.

It felt good to be at Val Halla again. I soaked in the smell of smoky buckskins and bread baking and enjoyed the cats lying comfortably on the woodpile, glad they weren't mittens. There were several new banty hens clucking about, but no pig. Bill and Laurie were glad to let me do the milking that week, and when I started along the snowy path toward the barn, covered with nanny berries and manure, Kimikoi playfully nudged and butted me as if she was happy to see me. I made a note in my journal that she had gotten fat. Mia was as sweet as ever, and it was a treat to do the milking and collect the eggs. I was grateful that Laurie was willing and able to haul the water up from the river, and didn't ask for help.

Bill invited me to join him to check his trap lines on snowshoes, so early one morning, before the sun was high enough to soften the snow, we set out heading downriver. I was slow—I had been on snowshoes only once before, and felt clumsy—but Bill was patient with me. As we traversed along the embankment, I struggled to keep from sliding or falling, and admired how easily Bill made his way across the crusty snow. We went about two miles south, as far as Johnson's place. In the distant meadow above the beaver wetlands, we spotted elk, and just above soared a golden eagle. When we approached the trap lines Bill pointed out beaver and otter signs, but neither had been caught. It was a spectacular day, and I was just as happy that we didn't find any trapped animals.

That night Laurie prepared a meal that included smoked ham from Woink. The meat was delicious but it brought back the memory of him as a lovely companion, and I felt a little pang of sadness as we enjoyed dinner.

For the five or six days that I visited, Ken and I shared the bedroom that had been mine, but our connection was purely emotional and did not exist in a physical realm; we spent our nights in bed talking quietly about our relationship to Bill, and our happiness that Laurie was in his life. We also shared our thoughts about Lana; I had stayed friends with her, but Ken had ended their relationship after their summer adventure. As we drew close, I welcomed his warmth, but I worried a little that he felt something beyond friendship—something I knew I could not fulfill. In my journal I wondered if he might have had deeper feelings for me, although I never had that conversation with him. Ultimately, I decided that he was honest and open enough to have said so if that was the case.

After getting this small glimpse of life at Val Halla during the winter, I thought that maybe it would have been tolerable. In many ways it did seem to be a relaxing time. Laurie was doing beautiful beadwork, making small pouches with scraps of buckskin and then sewing her beaded medallions on as decoration. She kept happily busy, and seemed at ease and so able to take on that life in a way that I never had. I considered whether I would have immersed so deeply in that winter quiet. I didn't know, but I felt sure that Laurie was much better suited for that life, and for Bill.

Bill with a trapped beaver
Photo credit: Laurie Wagner

All of the tension that I had known while I lived at Val Halla was gone now, replaced with a simple satisfaction that I had experienced such an amazing realm and could now enjoy it as an occasional visitor. My relationship with Bill was easier, as I had hoped it would be, and Laurie and I established a special connection because of our shared experience and deep understanding of life at Val Halla with Bill.

The morning I got ready to drive home, the departure was vastly different from my October exit with Joe and Flo. Bill encouraged me to stay in touch and said he was glad that I had made the trip. Laurie left the door open for me to visit any time, and I was glad to have a chance to share that world, even from a distance. Ken drove out the same day and followed me as far as the crossroad that would take him west to Spokane. We got out of our vehicles to share a hug before we parted ways and he encouraged me to write or visit, wherever his nomadic route would lead him, and I extended the same invitation.

An hour after I waved goodbye to Ken, I was sitting at the kitchen table with Joe and Flo in Bigfork, sharing tea and happy banter. They loved hearing about my road trip and the visit with Laurie and Bill. They had met Laurie and agreed that she could hold her own with Bill, and said they hoped he would treat her well.

I stayed with Joe and Flo for a couple of days before I headed home. I drove straight through the night in another snowstorm on two-way roads. By the time I reached Denver, I was exhausted and glad to be back home with Mom and Dad.

In a journal entry dated May 4, I noted that I was reevaluating my time with Bill, trying to sort emotions. I had been confused, I wrote, "because I knew that I loved him, but not in a way I expected . . . but because I cared, and had experienced his way of life, and, most likely, because I needed to love him, and knew, too, that he craved love." There was a kind of emotional freedom washing over me since Laurie had entered his world. "She is strong and brave, and very honorable," I wrote, and added, "she will fulfill Bill's dream, to a certain point, but he will never be very Indian-like, though he is most admirable."

It was an odd, small jab at Bill's large ego, but I no longer felt I had to put him on a pedestal or see him as anyone other than who he was. His skill, determination, and courage were impressive, but he was not superhuman. He was reverent about the natural world, but not humble. His inner landscape housed enough turmoil that it was hard for him to provide an oasis of peace for others.

I imagined that Bill thought I had somehow sold out my ideals and reentered a world he condemned and despised—the American capitalist culture—but I felt my path was to find my own way to survive in that world without losing grip on my values or giving in to a system I did not admire. I reflected on how the past year had offered me the chance to grow in a direction I never could have imagined, both physically and spiritually, and I felt especially grateful for the people in my life and how they'd helped me along the way.

CHAPTER THIRTY-SIX

*N*ot long after I got home I received a letter of acceptance to Colorado College. I was surprised and excited, and Mom and Dad were entirely relieved for me to have something concrete to move toward. In the meantime, my neighbor, HK, helped me land a job for the summer working for friends of hers who owned a private guest ranch in southwestern Colorado.

The position started at the beginning of June, and I drove seven hours to reach the magnificent ranch property, located high above Creede, Colorado. My job was to work with the kitchen crew and help clean the three or four guest cabins. The ranch had several horses, and we could fish or ride on days off. The Jersey milking cow had a new calf that I helped care for, and I had my own one-room cabin halfway around the lake, as well as an old jeep to drive back and forth—it was ideal.

But the situation with my brother-in-law was not. Since I had been home, my relationship with him had seemed to diminish and fade into the background, because there had been no opportunity for him to be alone with me. I hoped it would just disappear, but that summer he figured out a way to create a situation where he could be with me, and I entered a troubled place with him again. There were two nights that we spent alone together, and we had sex, but it was nothing like love. I felt lonely and ashamed, and knew that with intercourse, I had crossed a barrier; I was no longer a minor, and I felt responsible for how this would affect my family. I was angry with myself and with him. But he didn't seem to have any doubt, or remorse, or even emotion while we were together; it was as if he was disconnected from the reality of what we were doing and who I was to his wife and kids. I promised myself that this summer was the end of it but couldn't seem to muster any words to express that to him, which tacitly seemed to allow for some future encounter.

I thought I could shed the situation with my brother-in-law simply by entering a new realm at college, but he was still intent on pursuing a relationship with me. He came to find me at school soon after I started there—called my dorm phone and said he had some business nearby and would like to take me out for Indian food. *Okay*, I thought. This would be my chance to tell him this had to stop. Something had shifted during those first few weeks at college and I finally saw him as a predator. I didn't expect an apology, but I wanted some kind of admission of responsibility from him. My heart was aching for my sister and my niece and nephew.

At the restaurant, we made small talk. I couldn't see an opening, so I waited until he brought me back to the dorm and my room, where he made it clear he wanted to slip into the pattern he had established with me. When I told him no, he acted hurt with rejection, then slunk away like a naughty child who has been caught stealing. He never approached me again, and we never talked about it. It would become, over time, like a bad dream forgotten—one I'd never talk about with my sister until decades later.

Structure, challenge, and studies would help to steer me in a new direction—a place where I could delve into art, anthropology, Southwest studies, and much more. School life was demanding and rewarding, but my own tendencies and situations kept shifting under me like sand. I thought I should feel liberated now that I had distanced myself from the distress of trouble with male relationships, but instead I felt confused and vulnerable and didn't know what my role was with men.

In the years to come, my life would take on a form that was so unlike the shape it had held when I was at Val Halla; I went too far in the other direction and landed in a very unbalanced place, losing ground with pot smoking and alcohol. I'd thought I would be able to stay away from all of it, but the temptations that came with student life in the dorms, and my own weakness around pot, replaced my resolve.

Four years were wasted on a very negative relationship that left some scars. The confused mess of that involvement pushed my Montana connection to the back of my mind, even though I never let go of the memories or my musings about Bill, Laurie, Joe, and Flo. Laurie continued to write to me at college for a year or two, sharing news from a world she knew I could envision and appreciate. Her letters were full of anecdotes about the animals, especially Mia and Kimikoi. She let me know that Bill had to shoot Ahkee. Bill and Laurie were riding, and led the horses through a beaver pond. A sharp beaver stick gouged Ahkee as he lunged through the pond, and he was too badly wounded to survive. Woinks II and III were raised and butchered, lots of goats came and went, various visitors and apprentices made appearances, and life at Val Halla seemed vivid but removed. She told me about her trials and accomplishments with the challenges of chores, her love of the life at Val Halla, and her joys and occasional struggles in her relationship with Bill.

When Bill wrote, he described his gardens, hunting and setting traps, preparing buckskins, his adventures on horseback and animal sightings, fixing the barn, and the daily essence of life. His letters expressed a genuine and friendly voice of camaraderie; as gruff as he had often been while I was in his world, it seemed he cared. Maybe distance had something to do with his softer view of our time together. It was as though I was reading a story with many chapters in which I had once been a character but had since stepped away from the pages.

Eventually, the exchange of letters with Bill and Laurie stopped and I resigned myself to the understanding that that part of my life was The Past. Laurie and Bill eventually had to leave Val Halla—there may have been some issues between Bill and the land owners, since he was basically caretaking the property and had no ownership rights. Flo mentioned something about goats and damage. Sometimes connections fade and disappear into some storage place, to be drawn out when the time is right. Letters from Ken, Lana, and Bill's mother eventually stopped coming after I let too much time go by without responding, but I did continue to share notes with Joe and Flo at Christmastime.

After those few chaotic years, I graduated from college and moved to the East Coast with a partner to be near his family—the start of a new chapter. I continued to feel a righteous, heartfelt anger about the dark history of this country's treatment of Native Americans. As I grew older, I struggled to replace my impatient and critical attitude with humility and compassion, but the angst I voiced at seventeen about man's abuse of the environment persisted.

The urgency to act became more pressing with time, and as I emerged from my college years I realized it didn't make sense for me to hide and do nothing to help address these problems, large or small. I needed to find purposeful direction in the community where I lived; I could have a bigger impact on environmental issues as a team player. My first real work in this area was with other volunteers and nonprofit groups on waste reduction and sustainable energy projects, which proved empowering and brought me unexpected joy. Those efforts would lead me to a master's degree in environmental studies and a deeper understanding of the natural sciences. I went on to earn a certificate in natural science illustration, which allowed me to use my art to teach seeing/drawing from nature and, occasionally, produce educational materials.

Every cell of my body has continued to feel the pull of living close to the natural world. I have been fortunate to find a peaceful home with someone I love, in a small town near a big river in New England where I can walk to the post office, library, farmers market, and little grocery store as easily as I can step onto the trails in the woodlands and wetlands all around us. The sounds and smells of the woods fill me like the vapor of some powerful tonic. I walk and watch the light shift, the changes though the seasons, like a story unfolding. Although it is not the deep wilderness of Bill's Val Halla, on occasion I see beaver, bobcat, otter, and moose tracks, and there are black bears, coyotes, turkey, and deer in the woods and fields. It is a beautiful, special realm.

EPILOGUE

1987

I took a train from Montreal to Calgary, where I met Mom and Dad while they were on a fishing trip. We had a plan to drive to Denver to see family and friends, with some stops along the way. When we headed south out of Canada we turned west to drive through Glacier Park over the magnificent Going-to-the-Sun Highway that I first experienced with Bill and his parents the day we drove to Browning, Montana. That night we stayed at St. Mary's Lodge, one of the gorgeous early-1900s lodges one finds throughout the West built from massive logs and with a stone fireplace so big you could stand upright in it. The glacial lake next to the lodge was an eerie aqua color; I braved a six-second dip, but it was shocking.

The next day we drove out of the park through West Glacier, stopped at the Polebridge store, then headed up to Val Halla. Bill and Laurie were long gone, and a woman who was conducting a wolf study was living in the cabin. The property looked much like the place I remembered, except that it was naked: many of the pine trees had been destroyed by a beetle kill. And it felt empty without the animals and the red truck in the yard, or the fenced gardens full of showy turnip tops and pea vines. But the cabin, the barn, and even the water tank where I showered with Bill that first day after we swam across the North Fork of the Flathead were still there.

Some family members of one of the property owners were around, so we picnicked at a table outside one of the small cabins with them and then toured the homesteader's cabin. I wanted Mom and Dad to have a tangible picture and was eager to paint the scene for them, even though it was entirely different and felt spare inside the cabin without Bill's furs, antlers, and piano. As we walked around the property, I felt like my time there finally came into full view for them. This tank was our shower, I explained, recounting my first day there and the warmth after a chilling swim across the river. And here is where Woink loved to lie in the sun, and where he died. There is the old tractor . . . and look, this is the big stump we threw tomahawks into!

Visit to Val Halla with Mom and Dad in 1987

It seemed important to revisit those memories and places with my parents. They had lost lots of sleep over me, and occasionally reminded me of that. Now I could at least open a window for them to see into that part of my life that we had shared through letters. I wanted them to know how much I appreciated their gift of love and trust. They had been there to guide me through that time in Montana when I needed advice, and to provide me with the comfort of deep love. Even though I'd pushed hard against and even condemned the society they existed within, they'd given me space, confident that I could find a way to engage in the world without insisting that it had to be *their* world. Dad's joy in living had been an oasis when I felt lost. He'd taught me that our lives are made rich when we believe in goodness and give something back; he'd nudged me away from selfish tendencies. Mom had understood my passion for the environment and a simple lifestyle and trusted that I would find my way. She genuinely supported and appreciated the path I'd chosen.

In the afternoon we headed back down to the valley and stopped at the south end of Flathead Lake to check into our motel before heading over to see Joe and Flo, who had moved to a new community. It was my thirty-first birthday, and we planned to celebrate with dinner together.

"You little stinker, you still look eighteen!" Flo said by way of greeting. From Joe I got a big hug and happy grin.

They were just as pleased to see Dad and Mom again. They had first met my parents soon after I returned from Montana, when they came to Denver to visit their daughter. On another trip a few years after that, Mom and I drove to Montana to visit her cousin in Billings and we stopped to visit with Joe and Flo in Bigfork for a day or two. Mom and I even did a little target shooting on that trip, since we brought Pappy's old Remington pump-action .22. Mom was a darned good shot—and a little competitive.

1993

Bill was now in Wyoming. When I finally found out where he was living I sent a letter, and he wrote back. Laurie was no longer with him but he was still living off the grid, in a cabin on his own land. He described in detail his hand-wrought cabin and life with his dogs, horses, and gardens, and it was almost as if no time had passed.

Over the years I would receive many such letters off the old typewriter from Bill. Of course, he would include the occasional rant about politics or the state of the world. When I was first exposed to him, many of his predictions of demise due to the waste of resources and abuse of our planet rang true; I believed things would play out much as he described. I also appreciated his certainty and contentment about the life he had forged.

My short time with Bill at Val Halla reinforced what I already believed about living simply, gave me the strength and tools to understand a life without modern convenience, opened my senses, and cultivated in me a deep reverence for the natural world. That time would remain vivid, coloring the many other layers of my life—stitched and torn, patched and added to along the way.

Laurie and I reconnected as well in 1993, years after she had left Bill, while she was living with her husband on a Colorado ranch. We wrote and visited several times over the years, even joining a Colorado River raft trip with a few friends in 2000. After her husband died, she met and married a writer and musician, and they moved to Texas, where she tended her gardens, wrote, and spent as much time as she could absorbing the natural world. Laurie died from health complications in July of 2021. I will deeply miss that connection to our shared time at Val Halla, and her lovely spirit.

1996

Dad died in January of that year. He struggled with illness the last few years of his life but would love to have stayed around to enjoy the symphony, or fish on the Snake River, or host just one more party. I stayed with them in California, where they moved in 1976, to help Mom care for him for a spell in the last few months of his life. I was working on my master's thesis and tried to describe the gist of it to Dad.

"But what are you going to *do*, Babesy?" he asked one day while we sat out on the patio.

"Well, Dad, I want to start a consulting business to help people get rid of the toxic products they use around the house and use safer stuff, like baking soda and vinegar, to clean with . . ."

I explained some more about how I'd use my art background with natural science illustration. After I'd laid out my plans, Dad sat a moment, then nodded and said, "Oh, that sounds very good."

1997

Joe and Flo happily spent the last part of their lives back in Bigfork. When I called to chat one day in 1997, Joe said I'd better come visit since they weren't going to live forever. I'm glad I did, because it would be the last time I would get to Montana to see them and to visit Val Halla. Our time together was happy and sweet, and sprinkled with melancholy. We drove up the North Fork one day to picnic and spend a little time at Moose City.

The early August day was clear blue and bright, and Joe and Flo sat on the porch of their little cabin playing a few hands of gin rummy while I walked across the meadow to see where the cabin had been washed away by a flood earlier that year. The water had an orange tinge from a mine in Canada that had begun operating upriver from our homestead some years after I left, polluting the Flathead with effluent. Standing on the edge of the reconfigured river bank, I tried to remember where the cabin, garage, and pigpen had been, but was disoriented. In my mind I could picture the scene, but they were gone, and little of Val Halla remained except the barn and the old red tractor.

I sat on a stump above the washed-out river to draw and write down some thoughts, but I felt empty; after a little while, I walked back across the meadow to Joe and Flo. The three of us, walking slowly since Flo had lost some of her vision, wandered the path to the spring next to the small creek along the embankment where I had encountered the grizzly and her cub. I drank from the spring with the ladle that was still hanging there in the little structure. Someone's cache of canned beer was chilling in the cold water, and I grumbled. Flo agreed but reminded me that with more property owners and visitors to the area, it would never again be the remote and pristine place of my memories.

2009

Mom had a minor stroke in May, just before a trip I had planned with her to take a driving tour of western Colorado. She could no longer drive or hold cards for a game of bridge, so she decided she had lived the best of her life and faded peacefully, as was her wish. She planned her own memorial down to the brunch menu, which included chicken salad and Bloody Marys for her bridge friends. She also requested that the hospice chaplain read from Norman McLean's *A River Runs Through It* in place of anything religious. At the memorial, we all raised a toast to celebrate her indominable spirit.

After Mom died, a crack opened in the sealed box of my past experiences regarding my brother-in-law. I was afraid of what this might do to my family, but needed to share that history with them. They gracefully accepted the truth, and have negotiated this shift in our relationships with love and understanding. We now spend our time together with sincerity and compassion, quietly aware of the relief that comes from healing. I am deeply grateful for this resolution.

When I close my eyes and go back to Val Halla, I step into the cool brook and look up to see the grizzly sow just a few yards up the bank, the sun sparkling in her fur, her cub just behind her. That moment is forever etched in my mind. The insistent predawn wakeup call from Chanticleer floats into my head and I go through the routine of getting the woodstove lit and hot with a few pieces of kindling and just one match, turning the damper down, and feeling the chill disappear. Then I pick up the milk pail and head to the barn with Mia and Kimikoi and smell the warm milk as I squeeze Mia's teats—right, left, right, left—into the pail. Next, to the chicken coop to gather the eggs, then back to the cabin to stir the pot of grains I left cooling so I can feed

Woink, who is busy turning up the stone path just outside the woodshed in the morning sun. He sits down and waits for me to come out with his breakfast.

ACKNOWLEDGMENTS

To all of my family and friends who have shared this journey with me, thank you from the bottom of my heart. So many friends have been willing to hear my story along the way, and your generosity is boundless. I would like to especially thank the handful of readers who have given me their time, editing savvy, and important feedback, including Mary Burns, Susan Klann, Kira Kmetz, Lisa Connors, Barb Wheeler, John Bradley, and Roland Merullo. Special thanks to my She Writes Press editor, Brooke Warner, who had faith in me, and pushed me to write more deeply and create a story. Thanks, also, to my publication manager, Lauren Wise, for steering me through this process. My long-time friend and photographer, Amanda Merullo, made me laugh and captured a photo for my back cover. I am honored to have endorsements from fellow writers, Laura Waterman, Roland Merullo, Gretchen Cherington, and John Bradley.

Bill Atkinson gave me permission to publish his letters; this story would not exist without him. Laurie Wagner opened her heart to me about her time at Val Halla and urged me to tell my story. Lois Walker, who lives along the North Fork, provided information about the history of the Polebridge store and residents, and photos of the cabin being washed away in a flood.

Woink was there when I needed a hug, and thinking of him fills me with joy.

My husband, David Gordon, has encouraged and supported me every step of the way on this occasionally bumpy journey, and I am deeply grateful.

ABOUT THE AUTHOR

Photo credit: Amanda Merullo

Annie Chappell grew up in Denver, a fifth-generation Coloradoan. Her interests in anthropology led her to study ancient cultures, especially those of Native American and Mesoamerican peoples. She has always admired the drawings of naturalists like Audubon and Meriweather Lewis, and she now teaches others to draw from nature and better understand their world. She has a BA in Art from Colorado State University, a Master of Science in Environmental Studies from Bard College, and a Certificate in Natural Science Illustration from the Cary Institute. In 2004 she created a series of paintings of invasive species that was exhibited at the Denver Botanic Gardens, The Great Falls Discovery Center, Turner's Falls, MA, and the Fish and Wildlife Exhibit Hall, Hadley, MA. Annie is a passionate environmental advocate and works locally as a volunteer toward sustainability through waste reduction and non-toxic alternatives. On occasion she writes articles for the "Green Living" section of her local paper. She lives in a small town in Western Massachusetts with her husband. Together, they enjoy tending to their gardens and playing Old Time string band music with friends.

SELECTED TITLES FROM SHE WRITES PRESS

She Writes Press is an independent publishing company
founded to serve women writers everywhere.
Visit us at www.shewritespress.com.

Drinking From the Trough: A Veterinarian's Memoir by Mary Carlson,
DVM. 978-1-63152-431-8. The story of a suburban Chicago girl who
never expected to move "out West" and become a veterinarian, let
alone owner and caretaker of cats (many), dogs (two), and horses
(some with manners, some without) in Colorado, but did—and, along
the way, discovered the challenges, tragedies, and triumphs of lives,
both human and animal, well lived.

Last Trip Home: Story of an Arkansas Farm Girl by Wanda Maureen
Miller. $16.95, 978-1-63152-339-7. After growing up on a small Ar-
kansas farm in the 1940s and 1950s and struggling with poverty, her
father's lecherous grip, and a husband in the Klan, Grace Marie Hall
escaped to a life in California—but now her father has died, and she
returns to Arkansas for what she hopes will be her last trip home.

Mt. Moriah's Wake by Melissa Norton Carro. $16.95, 978-1-64742-138-
0. In this literary exploration of the incapacitating effects of grief and
guilt, a young woman returning home must face her past and the
skeletons in her small southern community—and come to terms with
her present life.

*Newcomers in an Ancient Land: Adventures, Love, and Seeking Myself
in 1960s Israel* by Paula Wagner. $16.95, 978-1-63152-529-2. After
leaving home at eighteen in search of her Jewish roots in Israel and
France, Paula learns far more than two new languages. To navigate
her new life, she must also separate from her twin sister and forge her
own identity.

*The Field House: A Writer's Life Lost and Found on an Island in
Maine* by Robin Clifford Wood. $16.95, 978-1-64742-045-1. When
Robin Clifford Wood stepped onto the sagging floorboards of Rachel
Field's long-neglected home on the rugged shores of an island in
Maine fifty years after Field's death and began dredging up the bril-
liant but largely forgotten writer's history, the journey took her far-
ther than she ever dreamed possible.